J. TERRY JOHNSON

Foreword By Sherri Coale

Two Parts Sunshine

The Life and Recipes of Marty Johnson

Two Parts Sunshine

Editing by Kylie Lyons
Cover and Interior design by Kandi Evans

Published in the United States of America

ISBN:978-0-615-35863-5

1.Biography/ Cookery
02.25.10

Dedication

This book is dedicated to an extraordinary group of women. They are the working force of Oklahoma Christian Women's Association: those who have been members in years past; those who hold membership in the organization today; and those who will become members in future years. They have made an enormous contribution to the development of a small Oklahoma college that has emerged as one of the nation's premier Christian liberal arts universities. The net proceeds from the sale of this book are pledged to support the many good works undertaken by the women of OCWA.

Acknowledgements

Some have found it amusing that a person who burns toast and is unable to scramble eggs in a frying pan could be so audacious as to write a cookbook. My answer is simple. I may not have what it takes to prepare good food in the kitchen, but I know good food when I taste it.

I come from a line of good cooks. My mother, Jeanne Johnson, and my grandmother, Ida Johnson, were good cooks. They didn't have all the modern appliances that adorn kitchens today, but they knew how to whip up a meal that could feed the family or half the neighborhood, and with plenty left over for second- and third-helpings.

My wife Marty is an excellent cook. She can turn grilled cheese sandwiches into a gourmet meal for two. Her mother, Mable Mitchell, was also a hospitable woman who prepared dishes according to that old-school of culinary thought—"a dash of this and a pinch of that." Whenever she was in doubt about a recipe, she would improvise and the results were astounding. Marty learned to study and follow recipes more carefully than her mother, but on occasion, she would revert to experimentation, ala Mable, and with similar, mouth-watering results.

Although most of the recipes in this book are those that Marty has acquired, adapted or invented on her own over our forty-six years of marriage, several friends and relatives, living and deceased, have also contributed their own special recipes and we gratefully pass them along to you. A bouquet of roses and kudos to the following contributors: Mable Mitchell, Jeanne Johnson, Ida Johnson, Jim and Sarah Maple, Brooks and Vickie Mitchell, Nancy Mitchell, Rita Brown, Hester Kelcy, Carrie Lou Little Davis, Lynda Scott, Gayla Peeples, Becky Johnson, Linda Offutt, Judy Standridge, and Betty Weissinger.

Once again, I am indebted to the professional staff at Tate Publishing for assisting me with the editing, layout, and cover design for the book. They published two previously released books, *Kirby* and *Cardinal Fever*. Kylie Lyons served as my editor and Kandi Evans arranged the layout and developed the graphic design for *Two Parts Sunshine*.

From our thirty-two years at Oklahoma Christian, Marty and I share the satisfaction of knowing that hundreds of students were well prepared for adulthood and for succeeding in their chosen professional careers. None is more representative of that on-going phenomenon where high school graduates morph into responsible professional adults than the experience of Sherri Buben Coale, who came to Oklahoma Christian in 1983 upon graduating from high school in Healdton, Oklahoma.

Sherri was a stellar member of the Lady Eagles basketball team in the mid-1980s and made the Dean's List at Oklahoma Christian, semester after semester. Now she has garnered nationwide acclaim for herself and the Women's Basketball Program at the University of Oklahoma where Sherri has served as the program's head coach since 1996. We salute her and express our special thanks for her taking the time to write the Foreword to *Two Parts Sunshine*.

Contents

Foreword by Sherri Coale 11

Two Parts Sunshine 15

A Mail-Order Bride 29

Getting Started in "Big D" 43

The House in the Woods 55

OCC's First Lady 67

The Green Herb 81

High Society 95

International Tour Hostess 111

Executive Director 123

Horseshoe Bay 135

World-Class Grandmother 149

Recipe Index 161

Foreword

"This little light of mine, I'm gonna let it shine. This little light of mine, I'm gonna let it shine. Let it shine, all the time, let it shine…"

That famous vacation Bible school song is what I think of when I think of Marty Johnson. I attended Oklahoma Christian College in the early 80's, and as a small town girl, OC was my window to the world. J. Terry Johnson was our University President, the purveyor of lofty dreams, the staunch dignitary who shuffled about campus looking serious and austere. He was the chapel speaker, the tie wearer, the guy who made the tough calls battened down behind the walls of the castle. He might have been larger than life had he not been married to a mighty mouse of a woman who was as real as sliced bread.

Marty Johnson was OC's campus matriarch. She stood about 5 foot nothing, a ball of endless energy and a 1,000 watt smile. She dressed impeccably, showed up incessantly, and entertained more than anyone I had ever known. She was famous for her cooking, especially her desserts as I recall, but what I most remember is her smile.

I ran into Marty at Chicago's O'Hare Airport back in the summer of 2009. I was recruiting; my son was with me, and we were starving. We jumped in line at a little make-shift deli near our gate, behind a lovely, little woman who was making excessive inquiries about the contents of the salads and the sandwiches on display. Fortunately, she kindly motioned for those of us in line behind her who were either sure of our order or not concerned in the least about its contents, to proceed in front of her. We quickly took her up on her offer, based mainly on the latter. As I rattled off our selection to the cashier, the petite, inquisitive woman grabbed my arm and exclaimed in a dripping Texas drawl, "Sherri Coale!! It's Marty Johnson!"

Of course it was. I hadn't seen her in 20 years, but I recognized her instantly. She still looked like she had just "stepped out of a band box," as my Granny used to say. (And while I don't really know the phrase's origin, I know exactly what it means. And that's exactly how Marty looked.) Her eyes still sparkled and her smile was just as wide and as perfectly painted as I recalled. She launched into fast conversation, gasped at my 'tall, handsome son', and generally made it seem as if we had last spoken on the previous Monday. Such is her gift.

When we walked away, my son said, "Who was that woman? She just might be the happiest person I've ever seen." And as I laughed, I couldn't help but think how little hyperbole there was in his succinct analysis.

Teams and companies and institutions alike eventually take on the demeanor of their leaders. Alas, Oklahoma Christian floated on the air of Marty Johnson. It was her spirit, her joy, her zest for life and all its little jagged pieces that gave our campus its heartbeat.

When you walked around on that hill where the wind blew right through you, you had a tendency to believe you could grow wings and fly. It was a place and a time where all things seemed possible. A whole lot of that climate came from her.

"…hide it under a bushel? No! I'm gonna let it shine! Let it shine all the time, let it shine!"

Marty was, and still is, a fantastic cook and a gracious hostess. While I know the recipes shared in this book are divine (I've tasted several and can vouch for the final product!), I'm convinced that the heart of the cook is where the real magic lies. And I feel absolutely certain that Marty would want you to smile while you stir.

Sherri Coale, Head Coach
Women's Basketball Team
The University of Oklahoma

Two Parts Sunshine

It must have been something like this: *one part clay, two parts sunshine, a touch of mischief, and a heart of gold.* That's the recipe God must have used when He made Marty.

Born in Tulsa, Oklahoma, during the last few months of World War II, Martha Susan Mitchell was the second child of U. S. Army Corps Captain Lloyd Brooks Mitchell and his beautiful wife, Mable Grace. Having endured the darkest days of the Dust Bowl as the teenage son of a sharecropper, and later as a young military officer who flew twenty-five successful missions over the war zones of Western Europe, Lloyd Mitchell was a survivor. He never forgot the struggles of his youth and taught his children valuable life lessons drawn from his own experiences in the parched Oklahoma cotton patches and in the navigator's seat of a B-17.

Martha's early years were filled with nomadic journeys, criss-crossing the nation as she followed her parents from Oklahoma to Washington, DC; to Oregon and Washington; and on to Minnesota and South Dakota. With older brother, Brooks, and younger sister, Sarah Ellen, Martha lived for a year on the renowned Rosebud Reservation in South Dakota. Lloyd had taken a job with the Bureau of Indian Affairs as a land appraiser. If Indian lands were bought or sold, Lloyd's job was to ensure that the Indian tribes and their individual members were treated fairly in the transactions.

Brooks and Martha–circa 1946

On the Rosebud, the Mitchells lived in a house that had been built for the Sioux's tribal nurse. The Mitchell children were considered to be "outsiders" on the reservation, and their parents cautioned them not to venture very far from home. Although curious about the Indian families who lived nearby in small homes or in primitive Native American tepees, Brooks and Martha heeded the gentle warning from their parents and did not make close friends with the Indian children.

There was no local church suitable for the Mitchells to attend, so Sunday worship services were conducted in their home. Mable would teach a Bible lesson to the children, Lloyd would read the Scriptures and offer a prayer, and the whole family would sing the first verses of familiar hymns such as "The Old Rugged Cross," "Guide Me O Thou Great Jehovah," or "Anywhere with Jesus." Mable longed for the fellowship of the 10th and Rockford Church of Christ in Tulsa, where she had attended as a child, but in the spirit of a pioneer woman, she made the best of the situation as it was.

Only Brooks and Martha were old enough to attend school. Sarah was still a toddler, four years younger than Martha, and not old enough for the public kindergarten class offered at the small elementary school north of the reservation. In a utilitarian wood-frame building divided into a few small classrooms, Martha began her formal education. She had above-average curiosity about learning and made a few new friends, but most of her free time was spent with her siblings at home on the reservation.

—

In early 1952, the Mitchells moved from the Rosebud to a community near Aberdeen, South Dakota. Lloyd and Mable located a comfortable house in the small town of Warner, where the whole family took a collective sigh of relief, delighting in a more liberated style of family life away from the isolation they felt on the reservation. Brooks and Martha were enrolled in the local elementary school, while Sarah and infant brother, David, the newest arrival in the Mitchell clan, kept Mable busy at home. Being the elder daughter at age seven, Martha became her mother's deputy assistant in caring for the baby and handling other household chores that were within her growing capability.

The Mitchell children were generally well behaved, but there were a few memorable incidents when stern discipline was required. One day when Martha had had enough of her older brother's taunting, she threw a pair of scissors that stuck in Brooks' forehead. The injury proved to be superficial, but Lloyd, usually a mild-mannered father, gave his daughter a spanking that she never forgot.

And there was the day Martha played beauty salon operator, chopping off her school chum's waist-long pigtail. Upon discovering the severed hair lying on the basement floor, the friend's mother let out a scream that was heard all over the neighborhood. She was furious with Martha and chased her all the way home. Mable administered the spanking that night.

One summer's afternoon, the Mitchell children and their Tulsa cousins, Linda Fay and Mary Lloyd Apple, spent a lazy day together at their grandparents' farm near Bixby, Oklahoma. A watermelon patch was brimming with melons that were ripening on the vine and would be ready for harvest within a few days. Without thinking of the consequences, Martha joined her brother and cousins in a testing party, cutting plugs out of the melons to see if they were ripe. Granddad Marvin Apple threatened to use his razor strop on the mischievous miscreants, but cooler heads prevailed.

No congregation of the churches of Christ existed in Warner or Aberdeen, so the family joined with two other Christian families to plant a church in Huron, South Dakota—81 miles from the Mitchells' home. They made that drive once a week for more than a year until other Christian families began moving into the Aberdeen area. When that occurred, Lloyd and Mable bid a tearful farewell to their church friends in Huron and joined with a few local families to establish a new congregation in Aberdeen—one that made for a much shorter commute.

In 1955, when Martha was ten and ready for the fifth grade, Lloyd accepted the Bureau of Indian Affairs' proposal that he move back to Oklahoma. The entire family welcomed the opportunity to move to a warmer climate where summer lasted much longer than the blink of an eye. They settled in Anadarko, a community that prided itself in being "The Indian Capital of the World." Martha attended grades five through eleven in Anadarko Public Schools, more years than she had lived at any one place in her entire life.

Martha–5th grade in Anadarko

Outside the classroom, Martha filled her spare time with a host of extra-curricular activities. She played the flute in the school band, and over the objection of her father's criticism of the skimpy outfit she was required to wear, she became a majorette in the Anadarko High School Marching Band. She amused herself for hours twirling her baton and, with knees lifted high, marched around her backyard to the famous chords of John Philip Sousa.

The rules of the house forbade Martha from wearing excessive makeup, but she didn't need glamour products to turn the heads of the boys at school. She had natural beauty that radiated from head to toe. Her brunette hair, often teased into a sizeable bouffant, adorned an angelic face that was brightened by her signature smile. Only five feet two inches on her tiptoes, smallest among her four siblings, she was a cover girl, waiting to be discovered by some teenage fashion magazine.

Boyfriends stood in line at the front door of the Mitchells' house on West Davis Street. There was Gene Hacker, the Baptist minister's son; Derrell Griffith, an outstanding athlete who later played Major League Baseball with the Los Angeles Dodgers; and the neighbor, Bob Miles, whose dad was a prominent physician in the Anadarko community. They all spent a few coins taking Martha to the movies and to the drive-ins for Coke dates.

In her junior year, and her final year at Anadarko High School, Martha was nominated Basketball Queen. Although popular among her peers, Martha knew that other girls whose parents belonged to the country club usually won these honors. However, she made friends easily and was naturally kind to everyone she met, treating people fairly regardless of their social or economic standing. Campaigning for the upset, Donnie Kuykendall, a popular African American athlete, and his younger brother, Mack, lobbied their classmates and carried the vote for their unheralded candidate. On that starry night, Martha wore the crown.

———

Mable Mitchell, Martha's mother, was a bright woman who had grown up on a farm. With five brothers and a younger sister, she had developed good homemaking skills at an early age. Already the mother to four children ages five through fourteen, she gave birth to a fifth, Mark, in October 1957, only a few months after moving the family to Anadarko.

Mable was a resourceful person who stretched Lloyd's modest paycheck each month to ensure there were enough groceries to feed a family of seven. One day a traveling salesman appeared at the Mitchells' front door, offering to sell a truckload of whale meat at a fantastic price. Mable decided she was up to the challenge and bought several pounds of the oily meat, placing most of it in her freezer. For weeks she disguised her entrees, preparing a variety of dishes and never revealing that the *mystery meat* was actually whale blubber.

Although she was never one to follow a recipe precisely, Mable was a gifted cook. She experimented with her cooking, occasionally displaying one of her favorite dishes at the Caddo County Fair, where she won a passel of blue ribbons. *A pinch of this and a dash of that* would always make her meals extra special. Martha had learned some rudimentary principles about cooking and hospitality from her mother, but over the years she crafted a style of entertaining that was all her own.

The Mitchell Family–circa 1960
Front row: David, Mark
Middle row: Sarah, Martha, Grandmother Hallie Apple
Back row: Brooks, Mable, Lloyd

Pinto Beans

Oklahoma Christian College Cafeteria Manager Glenn Nance always served pinto beans to the students on Saturdays. It was a hearty meal and good nutrition. Mable's beans were every bit as good, and it is her recipe that has been passed down through the family.

> 1 lb. dry pinto beans, picked over and rinsed
> 6 to 8 C. water mixed with chicken stock
> 1 onion
> 1 bay leaf
> 1 t. salt
> Pepper to taste
> Pieces of ham or a ham hock
> Cover beans with water and soak overnight.

The following day, drain and rinse beans.

Sauté onion and ham chunks in a heavy pot.

Add beans, water/broth, and other ingredients.

Bring to a boil and then lower the heat and allow to simmer for 2 to 3 hours, watching to see that water is added to keep beans from burning.

Angel Biscuits

This is a simple recipe that has been around for years. Mable could stir up these biscuits, iron a shirt, talk on the phone, and watch television all at the same time. It's that simple.

5 C. flour
¼ C. sugar
1 pkg. dry yeast
3 t. baking powder
1 t. baking soda
1 t. salt
2 C. buttermilk
1 C. shortening
1 stick unsalted butter, melted and cooled
Dissolve yeast in 2 tablespoons of warm water and allow to stand at room temperature.

Preheat oven to 450°.

Sift dry ingredients into a mixing bowl.

Cut in shortening until it makes a coarse meal of dry ingredients.

Add buttermilk and yeast and knead on a floured board until dough becomes smooth.

At this stage, you can refrigerate for later use or prepare immediately for baking. If you refrigerate, allow any dough you are ready to use to sit 1 hour at room temperature before baking.

Roll out dough to approximately ½ inch in thickness and cut with a biscuit cutter.

Place cut pieces 2 inches apart on a buttered baking sheet (or use parchment paper).

Brush pieces with melted butter and bake for 10 to 12 minutes at 450°.

Guacamole Dip

Mable submitted this recipe in 1974 for the Oklahoma Christian Women's Association's *Silver Anniversary Cookbook*. She perfected her guacamole dip while living five years in New Mexico.

    6 ripe avocados, chopped
    1 medium tomato, chopped
    2 t. lemon juice
    1 t. salt
    1 small onion, chopped
    2 T. mayonnaise
    4 drops Tabasco sauce

Place chopped items in blender with remaining ingredients and blend until smooth. Chill well before serving.

Strawberry Bread

Mable made this simple recipe, sometimes serving it as a dessert and at other times as breakfast bread. Marty often served strawberry bread whenever she hosted a brunch.

4 eggs
1½ C. vegetable oil
3 C. flour
1½ pkgs. frozen sliced and sweet-
ened strawberries, thawed
1 t. baking soda
1 t. salt
3 t. cinnamon
2 C. sugar
1 C. pecans, chopped
Grease and lightly flour two loaf pans.

Preheat oven to 350°.

Mix strawberries, eggs and oil into a large mixing bowl.

Sift dry ingredients into strawberry mixture.

Add pecans and blend well.

Pour mixture into loaf pans.

Bake for 1 hour at 350°, or until tester indicates cake is done.

Mable's Banana Pudding

Mable made many wonderful desserts, but her specialty was banana pudding. She didn't need a recipe–it was written on her heart.

> 1 pkg. instant vanilla pudding mix
> 1 can Eagle Brand milk
> 1 large carton of Cool Whip
> 2 boxes of Vanilla Wafers
> 5 or 6 bananas, sliced lengthwise, then cut in half

Prepare pudding according to instructions on box.

Add Eagle Brand milk to pudding mixture.

Fold in ⅔ of the Cool Whip.

Using a 9x13 baking dish or a glass rotunda bowl, layer half of the Vanilla Wafers, half of the banana slices, and half of the pudding mix. Repeat this layering pattern and top off with remaining Cool Whip. Sprinkle top with grated chocolate, or coconut, or Vanilla Wafer crumbs.

Peanut Brittle

This thin peanut brittle was a holiday favorite of the Mitchell family for many years, and it brought rave reviews from friends throughout Caddo County, Oklahoma.

    1 C. white sugar
    1 C. white Karo syrup
    ½ C. water
    1 T. butter
    2 C. raw peanuts
    1 t. vanilla
    1 t. baking soda

Prepare a buttered cookie sheet.

Boil sugar, syrup, and water until mixture forms a brittle thread in cold water (275° on a candy thermometer).

Add butter, peanuts, and vanilla, and cook until yellow-brown.

Remove from stove and stir in baking soda.

Pour immediately onto buttered cookie sheet and allow to cool.

A Mail-Order
Bride

Martha and her father had some serious discussions about her plan to graduate early from Anadarko High School. For most students, the senior year in high school is unlike any other, and Martha's parents were concerned that she may have been giving up more than she realized. But Martha held firm in her position, and since she had the necessary credits to graduate, she walked across the stage in May of 1962, receiving her high school diploma at the close of her junior year.

The ambitious young graduate was not quite as successful in the second part of her plan. Most of her friends were planning to attend the University of Oklahoma in Norman or Oklahoma State University in Stillwater. Martha preferred OU but would have settled for OSU, where Brooks was pre-enrolled for his sophomore year. Her father explained matters to her this way: "You may attend either

OU or OSU, but if you want your mother and me to help you pay the tuition and fees, you will attend Oklahoma Christian College in Oklahoma City." Reluctantly, she packed her bags and made plans to enroll at OCC in the fall of 1962.

Having served the previous summer as a counselor at Camp Wyldewood near Searcy, Arkansas, Martha enjoyed meeting new Christian friends. To her delight, attending college with five hundred Christian classmates was almost as much fun as being at camp. The challenge of taking college-level courses added a new dimension to the mix, but she was much more comfortable at OCC than she had originally imagined.

When Fish Week was conducted in early September, she was among the most popular targets for the upperclassmen's jokes and pranks. She proudly wore the infamous onion strung around her neck and sang nursery rhymes while standing on a chair in the cafeteria. At the end of the week, she had won the hearts of her fellow students and was one of the best-known freshmen on campus.

The fall term brought Martha new challenges, new friends, and a new name. One of her new friends was Marty Smith, an attractive coed who liked to laugh and have fun. She and Martha ran with some of the same friends, and after a few weeks the two freshmen became known as the "two Martys." From that curious happenstance, Martha accepted her new nickname, albeit somewhat reluctantly, and soon only her family and friends from Anadarko remembered her as Martha.

Marty's roommate in Women's A dorm was Arthena Stanley, a freshman from Tecumseh, Oklahoma. Arthena was a gifted student with good study habits, which made it easier for Marty to take her classes seriously. To the delight of her parents, Marty made all A's and B's in her first semester courses.

As is usually true for college freshmen, Marty had to learn the art of managing her time. Classes were spread out during the day, and extracurricular activities chewed up many hours of the young coed's free time. Young men called regularly at the women's residence hall, asking for weekend dates. She had no problem keeping her social calendar full.

Midway through her second semester, an upperclassman from Missouri called, asking that Marty join him for a Coke at the student center. She had met Terry Johnson once before. In fact, they had double-dated in the fall—each with a different partner. From this seemingly insignificant incident, a romance blossomed that continued throughout the spring term, was interrupted for three months during the summer, and renewed itself when classes resumed in September.

—

The fall of 1963 was filled with heartache and tragedy. A car-train accident occurred the night before classes were to begin in September, killing four Oklahoma Christian students plus the wife and child of OCC Vice-President Phil Watson. The student driving the car was Jerry Wheeler, a senior Bible major from Wichita, Kansas, and Terry's roommate.

The campus community was in a state of shock. Students and faculty drew upon their inner strength to find comfort in the midst of this tragic occurrence. In addition to handling her own grief, Marty shouldered as much of Terry's personal loss as she could. The two became an inseparable pair on campus, always together in the library, the student center, and at morning chapel.

Two months later, President John F. Kennedy was assassinated in Dallas. The entire nation was on its knees, mourning the loss of its charismatic leader. Intense personal sadness was the emotional motif of the day.

Nonetheless, there were at least two occasions during the fall that brought Marty exceptional joy. In November the student body elected her homecoming queen–a distinct honor for any coed, but especially for a sophomore. In keeping with OCC's tradition, the coronation was conducted during halftime of the homecoming basketball game in the campus gymnasium, known affectionately as "the Barn." Marty, standing with her attendants and their escorts, was the essence of regal grace and beauty. Her smile brightened every corner of the gloomy old Barn.

Marty–homecoming queen at Oklahoma Christian College in 1963

The second happy event caught Marty totally by surprise. Over the Christmas break Terry took Marty to Springfield to meet his parents. On the return trip to Oklahoma, Terry pulled his car to the shoulder of the Will Rogers Turnpike and proposed marriage, offering Marty an engagement ring and a pledge of his eternal love. She shed a few tears, slipped on the diamond ring, and a wedding was penciled in on the calendar for May 2, 1964. It would occur three weeks prior to Terry's graduation and on the same day as Lloyd and Mable's twenty-second wedding anniversary.

The wedding was conducted in the Anadarko Church of Christ–a building that later became a Sears Catalog Store, giving rise to the line that Marty may have been a "mail-order bride." Darvin Keck, an OCC professor officiated; Marty's sister Sarah was maid of honor, and Terry's brother Tim was the best man. The reception was held in the backyard of the home owned by the Mitchells' neighbors, Paul and Clara Keyes.

Sarah (Maid of Honor), Marty and her mother Mable prepare for the wedding–May 2, 1964

Because there were three weeks left in the academic trimester, the honeymoon was packed into twenty-four hours. The newlyweds enjoyed dinner Saturday night at Sleepy Hollow, a popular Oklahoma City restaurant that specialized in steaks and pan-fried chicken, served family-style with mashed potatoes, green peas, and baskets filled with homemade biscuits. They spent one night in the

Howard Johnson Motel on Lincoln Boulevard, and then returned to Edmond to finish the academic term.

When finals were over, Marty and Terry moved to Springfield, Missouri, for the summer. Terry ran a sales route for Swift and Company and preached for the Shell Knob Church of Christ. Marty worked in the credit department at Heer's—a well-known department store in downtown Springfield. They lived in an un-air-conditioned one-bedroom apartment where most evening meals were cooked on an outdoor charcoal grill.

Marty's cooking skills were just developing, but she wasn't afraid to entertain guests, even with her limited space and experience. Jim and Ida Johnson, Terry's grandparents who lived in Springfield, came to dinner one evening. Granddad Johnson swore that his new granddaughter-in-law's biscuits were the best he had ever eaten. Later he was told the secret—Martha Johnson had used a package of Martha White's Biscuit Mix. "Martha White. Martha Johnson. What's the difference? They're still the best biscuits I have ever eaten," proclaimed Marty's newest culinary admirer.

While living in Springfield, Marty collected recipes from her mother-in-law, Jeanne Johnson, who was also an excellent cook. The Johnsons always had a garden that provided fresh produce throughout the summer and into the early fall. Homegrown green beans and ears of corn directly from the stalk were staples in their summer diet. So was homemade ice cream, which Terry's father, Clifford Johnson, made with an old wooden freezer that he cranked by hand.

The summer passed quickly for the newlyweds. In late August, Marty and Terry loaded their possessions into their small sedan—an un-air-conditioned stick-shift Dodge Dart—and made the long trip south to Dallas, where Terry was pre-enrolled in Southern Methodist University's College of Law. New adventures awaited the young couple in "Big D."

Pot Luck Hamburger Casserole

This dish is ideal for a church "pot luck" and will keep well in the freezer. It was a favorite recipe of Jeanne Johnson, Marty's mother-in-law.

    1 lb. lean ground beef
    2 T. butter
    1 t. salt
    1 can (8 oz.) tomato sauce
    1 C. creamed cottage cheese
    1 C. sour cream
    1 green onion, chopped
    1 can sliced mushrooms
    8 oz. noodles, cooked
    2 oz. sharp cheddar cheese, grated

Grease a 9x13 baking dish.

Preheat oven at 350°.

Brown meat in butter and salt lightly.

Add tomato sauce and allow to simmer for 5 minutes.

Combine cottage cheese, sour cream, onion, mushrooms, and cooked noodles in a mixing bowl.

Alternate layers of meat sauce and noodle mixture in 9x13 baking dish.

Top with grated cheese.

Bake 30 minutes at 350°.

Sweet Potato Casserole

Marty's favorite vegetable is sweet potato. She grew up eating them fresh from her grandparents' garden. Here's a holiday favorite for yam lovers.

3 lbs. yams
½ lb. butter
¾ C. brown sugar
Nutmeg
1 T. rum
1 t. vanilla
½ t. almond extract
4 eggs
1 C. half 'n half

Grease a 9x13 baking dish.

Preheat oven to 350°.

Peel and slice yams.

Boil in lightly salted water; drain.

Mash cooked yams with butter.

Add other ingredients and continue to mix.

Pour mixture into 9x13 greased baking dish.

Pat with more butter and bake 20 to 30 minutes at 350°.

Sprinkle top with chopped pecans and/or mini marshmallows.

Brown under oven broiler for 2 minutes.

Grandmother Johnson's Red Hot Apples

Anytime the Johnson family got together in Springfield for a meal you could be sure that Grandmother Ida Johnson would bring the red hot apples. And if dinner was at her house, there would be three meat entrees, four vegetables, two salads, hot rolls, two different kinds of pie, and a freshly baked cake.

3 C. sugar
3 C. water
2 small pkgs. red hot candies
12 to 15 small apples, peeled and cored
Brown sugar
Raisins
Pecan or walnut pieces
Butter, melted
Pineapple juice

Preheat oven to 350°.

Combine sugar, water, and candy into a saucepan and bring to a boil to make syrup; allow to cool.

Place candy mixture in a 9x13 baking dish and add apples to mixture (should come approximately half way up the side of apples).

Cook slowly in oven, turning occasionally, until apples are deep red in color. Place apples on cookie sheet to cool.

Combine brown sugar, raisins, nuts, butter, and pineapple juice to create consistency of paste (not dry and not soupy); stuff cored apples with this mixture and reheat until stuffing becomes melted into apples before serving.

Gumdrop Bars

These chewy bars provide a delicious alternative to cake and brownies and are especially good for holiday entertaining.

BARS
4 eggs
2 C. brown sugar
2 T. cold water
1 t. cinnamon
½ t. salt
2 C. flour
½ C. pecans, chopped
1 C. spiced gumdrops, cut into little pieces (use scissors dipped in flour)

ICING
3 T. butter, melted
2 T. orange juice
1 t. orange rind, grated
1 C. powdered sugar

Grease 9x13 baking pan, and dust with flour.

Preheat oven to 350°.

Beat eggs well.

Add sugar and water.

Mix flour, salt, and cinnamon.

Sprinkle part of flour mixture on nuts and candy.

Add rest of flour mixture to eggs and sugar.

Fold in floured nuts and candy.

Spread thin in greased and floured 9x13 pan.

Bake at 350° for 30 minutes (do not over bake).

Mix icing ingredients and spread on cake while hot.

Allow cake to cool (but not completely) before slicing into bars.

Store in an air-tight container.

Jeanne's Pecan Tassies

Marty's mother-in-law, Jeanne Johnson, was an excellent cook whose recipes bore considerable influence from the South. With a sister living in Dallas and a brother in Baton Rouge, Jeanne found many ways to use pecans in her recipes.

1 C. all-purpose flour
3 oz. cream cheese, room temp
1 stick margarine, room temp
⅔ C. pecans, chopped
¾ C. light brown sugar
1 egg
1 t. vanilla extract
1 T. soft butter

Preheat oven at 325°.

Cut cream cheese and margarine into flour and mold into balls.

Shape balls to fit into a 24 mini-muffin pan.

Stir pecans, brown sugar, egg, vanilla extract, and butter. Blend well.

Use teaspoon to drop filling into shells.

Bake for 25 minutes at 325°.

Clifford's Homemade Ice Cream

Marty learned from her father-in-law, Clifford Johnson, that the key to making homemade ice cream with firm texture is two-fold: 1) use a freezer with a wooden bucket and a strong motor; and 2) pack the ice cream for at least three hours before serving.

>   2 C. sugar
>   6 eggs
>   1 can Eagle Brand milk
>   1 pint half 'n half
>   1 t. salt
>   1 T. vanilla
>   Whole milk

Use Cuisinart or blender to blend sugar, eggs, Eagle Brand, and half 'n half.

Fold in salt and vanilla.

Pour mixture into pre-chilled canister.

Insert paddle and add whole milk to the fill line.

Churn until motor stops or begins to labor.

Remove paddle, place foil and lid on canister, and pack with more ice and salt for three hours before serving.

Getting Started
in "Big D"

The four years Marty spent in Dallas were not exactly what she had pictured for her first years of marriage. Terry was totally absorbed in his legal studies at Southern Methodist University and in leading the youth group at the Walnut Hill Church of Christ. He had charted a meaningful course for himself, but his new bride was less sure about her own future.

Having just turned nineteen, Marty was only a year or two older than some of the senior high students at the church. She was a magnet for the teenage girls who thought of her as a role model. They loved to come by Marty's apartment and help her make cookies or prepare a meal for a needy family. She quickly became an integral part of Terry's work in youth ministry.

Knowing that she would have to place her own collegiate career on hold, Marty began searching for a full-time job. Within a week of her arrival in Dallas, she applied for a position with Texas Instruments, the huge semi-conductor manufacturer that employed thousands of people living in the sprawling Dallas-Ft. Worth metroplex. The TI Publications Department had an opening for a typist who had experience using the IBM Executive Typewriter and its complicated new feature called "proportional spacing." This keyboard element produced a crude form of justified margins that made the TI publications appear to have been type-set at a print shop. Since Marty had taken a typing course at Oklahoma Christian during the spring term, she was somewhat acquainted with the IBM Executive Typewriter and presented herself as being qualified for the position. With those credentials, and her naturally spunky disposition, she got the job.

Marty's fashionable look in Dallas–circa 1967

For the first two years, Marty was the primary breadwinner for the newlyweds. Money was incredibly tight. Terry earned only fifteen dollars per week at the church–hardly enough to cover out-of-pocket costs the couple incurred while working with the youth group.

Most meals that Marty prepared were simple. Sandwiches went into lunch sacks, and casseroles were prepared for the evening suppers at home. When they did eat out, Marty and Terry were fond of the El Fenix Mexican chain because it allowed a 15 percent discount to preachers who ate at their restaurants on Sundays.

The Johnsons also ate frequently at Wyatt's Cafeterias, a Dallas chain where two of the Walnut Hill elders were employed in the executive offices. Lynn and Barbara Packer and James and Betty Muns invited Terry and Marty to stay in their elegant homes and care for their children while the parents were away on week-long trips. They paid the Johnsons for the childcare service with coupon books from Wyatt's.

Walnut Hill was an affluent church, and the ladies were keenly aware of the latest fashion trends. Several women at the congregation actually had careers as professional models at the local Apparel Mart. At the close of each market, Sunday-morning worship services would feature the "best of show." Marty had no resources to keep pace with the trend-setters, but she took her cues from what they were wearing and found her own version of those clothing styles at Sanger's or Titche's, where the price tags on her favorite line of clothing, Bobbie Brooks, were more in keeping with her modest budget.

—

During their years in Dallas, the Johnsons lived in three different one-bedroom apartments. The first was east of North Park Mall, near the intersection of Park Lane and Greenville Avenue. Although well located for commuting to Texas Instruments and SMU, it was farther from the church and the many activities that were planned with the youth group. After the first six-month lease was up, Marty and Terry moved to a newer set of apartments on Hidalgo Street, south of the church building, between Marsh Lane and Webb's Chapel Road.

The third apartment unit was in a newer complex on Parkridge Street, immediately north of the intersection of Marsh and Forest Lanes. Here the Johnsons lived next door to two friends from Oklahoma Christian College–Bill and Julia Goodwin. Bill was full-time youth minister for the Northside Church of Christ, which was only a few blocks from the Walnut Hill church. Bill and Terry had played on the baseball team at OCC and shared much in common with their work in youth ministry.

Marty handles her evening chores in a one-bedroom Dallas apartment

One evening, well past bedtime, Julia telephoned her neighbors, pleading for the Johnsons to come next door. Upon entering the front door, it was apparent that the commotion was in the kitchen, where a small field mouse was cornered near the baseboard of the cabinets. Bill had a broom and was yelling at the intruder as if the petrified rodent could understand every word he was saying.

Before the incident ended, both Bill and Terry were up on the kitchen cabinet tops trying to coax the mouse out through the front door. It finally fell upon Julia and Marty to capture the critter under a pail and remove him from the premises. Both men spent weeks trying to convince their spouses that they had no fear of a little field mouse, but, to their chagrin, the women knew who had been brave for ridding the apartment of the helpless rodent.

—

Having never had a real honeymoon, Marty and Terry made a long automobile trip in the summer of 1967 to Montreal, Quebec, where they attended the internationally acclaimed Expo '67. Fashioned along the lines of a world's fair, Expo '67 was a stunning display of futuristic prognostications supported by examples of the latest technology that cut across myriad commercial markets. Marty especially enjoyed perusing the corporate-sponsored booths forecasting miraculous advancements in home appliances.

The Johnsons stayed in quaint bed-and-breakfast homes throughout New England, visiting Boston and Vermont before crossing the Canadian border. On their return to the States, they indulged one another's fantasies: Terry agreed to spend a romantic day viewing the mighty Niagara Falls with Marty; she consented to make a detour to Pittsburgh so that Terry could watch his beloved St. Louis Cardinals play a baseball game at Forbes Field.

Terry extended his three-year program at SMU's Law School by one semester so that he could work as a legal intern for Otis Engineering. One of the deacons at the Walnut Hill church, Robert H. Davis, Jr., hired Terry with the thought of the young law student eventually becoming a permanent employee of the Halliburton subsidiary. Marty left her job at Texas Instruments in order to take three classes at North Texas State University in Denton. During the year, she became pregnant with the couple's first child.

Jennifer Jeanne Johnson was born June 13, 1968, in Presbyterian Hospital on Thursday of Walnut Hill's Vacation Bible School. Mother and daughter handled their respective roles beautifully. A new generation was ushered into the world, and the proud parents began reading manuals on "How to Care for a Baby."

Although born in Texas, Jennifer was destined to have an Oklahoma childhood. Dr. James O. Baird had asked Terry to return to Oklahoma Christian College in the fall of 1968 to teach several courses and serve as the College's Staff Counsel. A part-time youth minister position was also open with the Wilshire Church of Christ in Oklahoma City. Raymond Kelcy, chairman of the Bible faculty at OCC, was the pulpit minister at Wilshire. Terry agreed to accept both positions, and the Johnsons moved to Oklahoma City in August 1968.

Marty anticipated a fresh start in new surroundings. She was ready for the challenges of motherhood, the completion of her college degree, and the purchase of a home she could call her own. The years in Dallas had been fruitful but stressful. Now she longed for a quieter and more simplified lifestyle.

Marty and her daughter
Jennifer Jeanne - 1968

Swedish Meatballs

When Jennifer and Jill were small, this was a meal Marty knew they would eat and enjoy. Swedish meatballs also graced many of her buffet tables for campus guests.

1½ lbs. ground beef
2 eggs, slightly beaten
1 small onion, chopped
1 t. salt
1 t. Worcestershire sauce
½ C. rice, cooked
½ can Cream of Celery soup
1 cup whole milk
Dash of pepper

Mix beef, eggs, onion, salt, Worcestershire sauce, and rice in a mixing bowl.

Form into small balls (ping-pong size).

Heat a small amount of shortening in a large skillet; when hot, brown meatballs.

Drain grease and add soup, milk, and pepper; bring to a boil.

Reduce heat and allow to simmer about 30 minutes.

Serve over rice or egg noodles.

Sloppy Joes

Jennifer and Jill are embarrassed that this recipe is in this book. When you have fed as many college students as Marty did over the years, knowing how to make Sloppy Joes is essential. Besides, it is one of my favorite "comfort foods."

1½ lbs. ground beef
½ C. onion, chopped
1 C. celery, chopped (optional)
2 T. vegetable oil
2 T. brown sugar
1½ t. salt
½ bottle chili sauce
2 T. apple cider vinegar
¼ C. green pepper, chopped (optional)
Hamburger buns

Using a frying pan, brown beef, onion, and celery in the oil.

Add remaining ingredients and simmer until mixture begins to thicken.

Remove from heat and serve on buns as a sandwich or open-faced.

Picnic Potato Salad

Most good cooks have a favorite recipe for making potato salad, but Marty's offering at the church's pot-luck luncheon is exceptional.

> 2 lbs. potatoes, boiled, peeled,
> and cut in ¾-inch cubes.
> 1 T. red wine vinegar
> ½ t. salt
> ½ t. ground black pepper
> 3 boiled eggs, diced
> ½ C. Hellmann's Mayonnaise
> 2 T. mustard

Place warm potato cubes in a medium bowl.

Sprinkle potatoes with vinegar, salt, and pepper.

Mix in remaining ingredients.

Refrigerate until ready to serve.

Taste for flavor and adjust seasonings if necessary.

Texas Pound Cake

There are many cakes more exciting than an everyday pound cake, but this one is exceptional. While living in Dallas, Marty made it her dessert of choice for family and guests. A special treat is the tasty crust that forms on top.

    3 C. sugar
    3 C. flour
    1½ C. Crisco
    8 eggs
    3 t. lemon extract
    2 t. vanilla

Heavily grease a cake tube pan.

Preheat oven to 325°.

Cream Crisco, sugar, and add eggs one at a time.

Add flour, lemon extract, and vanilla.

Spoon into greased cake tube pan.

Bake for 1 to 1½ hours until cake tester comes out clean.

Remove from oven and allow to stand 15 minutes before gently removing cake from the pan.

Texas Chocolate Sheet Cake

Everyone has access to this recipe or one similar. For years Marty rarely attended a picnic or potluck dinner without whipping out a chocolate sheet cake. This version came from her days in Dallas.

CAKE
1 stick margarine
½ C. Wesson Oil
4 T. powdered cocoa
1 C. water
2 C. flour
2 C. sugar
½ C. buttermilk
2 eggs, beaten
1 t. baking soda
1½ t. vanilla

ICING
1 stick butter
4 T. powdered cocoa
4 to 6 T. milk
1 box powdered sugar
1½ t. vanilla
1 C. pecans, chopped

Grease and dust a 9x13 cake pan with flour.

Preheat oven to 350°.

In a saucepan, bring margarine, Wesson Oil, cocoa, and water to a rolling boil; remove from heat.

Mix sugar and flour in a large mixing bowl.

Pour the cocoa mixture into sugar mixture and stir until well blended.

Mix buttermilk, eggs, soda, and vanilla and fold into cake batter.

Pour into a greased and floured 9x13 pan and bake for 20 to 25 minutes at 350°.

Begin making icing 10 minutes before cake is finished baking.

Mix butter, cocoa, and milk in a saucepan and bring to a boil.

Remove from heat and add powdered sugar, vanilla, and pecans.

Beat well and spread icing on hot cake as it comes out of oven.

The House in the Woods

Upon moving to Edmond, Oklahoma, the Johnsons bought their first home–an 1100-square-foot three-bedroom brick house located one mile west of the OCC campus. The equity required to purchase the residence on NE 139th Street was a meager $250. Although small, the house was so much larger than the one-bedroom apartments the couple had grown accustomed to in Dallas.

Two new arrivals quickly made the new quarters even smaller than they had seemed before. Marty's younger brother David had not adjusted well to his parents' move from Oklahoma to Albuquerque, New Mexico. In the fall of 1969, he returned to Oklahoma for his senior year, attending Edmond Memorial High School and staying in one of the Johnsons' tiny bedrooms. A few months later, Marty gave birth to her second daughter, Emily Jill, on April 15,

1970. The Johnsons urgently began their search for a house that offered the family more room.

Marty enrolled in classes at Oklahoma Christian College, intending to graduate within two years. She majored in English Education with certification to teach at the secondary level. She was diligent in her studies, attending classes regularly, and even took one of her final exams the day before she gave birth to Jill. A stressful semester of student teaching at Eisenhower Middle School, however, prompted her to consider new types of employment upon finishing her degree. She graduated with honors from Oklahoma Christian in 1971–nine years after she had enrolled as a freshman.

Terry passed the Oklahoma Bar Exam and began handling a few legal cases for friends and referrals. Marty, equipped with her own reconditioned IBM Executive Typewriter, was Terry's legal secretary. There were a few years where the legal fees they collected surpassed Terry's salary at the College. They saved the spare income and bought a two-and-a-half-acre lot in a new subdivision off Memorial Road, about a half mile east of the College.

W. T. (Taylor) Carter was an elder of the Edmond Church of Christ and a former business instructor at Oklahoma Christian College. He also built custom homes in the Edmond area. The Johnsons contracted with Carter to build their "dream home" on their newly acquired acreage. He patiently helped the couple work through the tedious process of making choices as they fashioned a comfortable four-bedroom brick home with a rear-entry garage and adorned with stylish wood-shake shingles. It was everything the young couple could possibly want.

Well, almost everything. There was not a stick of furniture in the living room, nor was there any furniture in the formal dining room. There were no flowers, no lawn, and no landscaping. All who came to the front door had to make their own path as there was no sidewalk to lead them from the unpaved driveway to the front porch. It

Marty, wearing a skirt Mable made from scraps of her own out-dated
dresses, and Terry attending an OCCWA function–circa 1970

was as if someone had begun a house and then ran out of money;
and for all practical purposes, that was exactly what had happened.

One day Marty experienced a terrifying occurrence at the house.
She called Terry at his campus office and insisted that he come home
immediately. An unidentifiable critter was in the house, and Marty
had it trapped in the master bathroom.

Upon arriving home, Terry assured his wife that everything
was going to be all right. He then warily poked his head into the
bathroom to discover that a squirrel, posing as a drowned rat, was
huddled in a corner next to the bathtub. The unwelcomed intruder
had dropped down through one of the vents on the roof and had
come up into the commode, gasping for air. With a broom and a
little coaxing, Terry helped the squirrel stagger out of the bathroom,
scurry across the bedroom floor, and jump out the open door into

the backyard. Mr. Carter had some screens put on the roof vents the very next day.

—

Living on acreage offered the possibility of having pets. Marty's parents had bought the lot north of the Johnsons, and Lloyd had purchased a small white gelding for his grandchildren's amusement. Jennifer and Jill were too small to ride alone, but they looked forward to pony rides led by their dad or granddad.

One Christmas, the Johnsons were going to make the holiday trip to Springfield to visit Terry's family. Marty had been negotiating with a former neighbor on 139th Street to buy a puppy from her Cocker Spaniel's litter. It would be the perfect surprise for the girls' Christmas. The trick was how to get the puppy to Springfield without spoiling the Christmas surprise for the girls. Using extended naptimes and a couple of sheets to screen the secret passenger from view, the mission was accomplished. Taffy, a blonde Cocker puppy, was an armful of excitement for the girls on Christmas morning.

Jennifer and Jill–circa 1974

Other than the legal typing she did from home, Marty did not try to work outside the house while the girls were pre-school age. Nothing had higher priority for her than her family. She did become active in the Wilshire chapter of the Oklahoma Christian College Women's Association and participated in their fund-raising events.

Also at the Wilshire church, Marty helped Terry host some of the youth events, but her heart was especially sensitive to the need of developing a curriculum for the toddlers–nine months to three years old. She helped others to inaugurate a new program called "cradle roll," placing infants in jumper seats arranged in a semi-circle before the teacher. Each Sunday morning, while seated on the carpeted floor, she taught Bible lessons and sang beautiful songs for the children to learn. The program was an instant success.

Raising two pre-school daughters, completing a college degree, and making a host of appearances for church and college functions made it difficult for Marty to develop much time for herself. Upon the recommendation of some friends, she joined a tennis league that played on indoor courts at the home of Betty Trice, a friend who lived in Edmond. Marty's game was good, and she found the social stimulus relaxing. She made new friends who demanded nothing of her except to enjoy a game of tennis once or twice each week.

Marty takes a break from her tennis practice session

In Dallas, while living in apartments, Marty had begun to entertain couples and small groups in her home, but she began to ratchet up the frequency of her hospitality upon moving into the new house in the woods. Church groups from Wilshire and small clusters of guests from the College were entertained with meals and rounds of the popular domino game, "42." Marty had learned to play "42" from her parents and her grandparents, Jim and Lina Mitchell, who lived in Rogers, Arkansas.

Among her favorite "42" guests were Raymond and Hester Kelcy. Although separated in age by a generation, Raymond Kelcy, the venerable chairman of OCC's Bible faculty, and Marty had excellent chemistry when they were partners at the "42" table. Both were savvy competitors, playing the game with skill and finesse. Their only weakness was a propensity to overbid their hands.

One night, the Kelcys came over for dinner and a round of "42." Raymond and Marty were partners and had been "bidding 'em up" from the very first hand. Hester and Terry played the game much more conservatively, often "sandbagging" the bid by passing unless they had an unusually strong hand. After Raymond and Marty had failed to make several high bids, Hester said, "Terry, I think we can beat these two if we will just resist the temptation to make a bid."

Little could Marty have known what lay ahead of her when it came to entertaining in her home. Whether hosting a birthday party for one of her daughters or entertaining the Endowment Committee of the OCC Board of Trustees, she honed her skills of making guests feel comfortable. She borrowed recipes from friends and family and began collecting books and articles about cooking. It was if she were destined for something great in the world of home entertainment.

Four years into his work with Oklahoma Christian College, Terry was named Vice President and, a year later, Executive Vice President. Marty and the girls could not possibly have imagined how their entire world was about to turn upside down.

No-Peek Beef Stew

Hester Kelcy introduced Marty to this recipe. It is a great winter dish and easy to prepare.

> 3 lbs. lean stew meat
> 2 medium onions, quartered
> 1 C. celery, chopped
> 8 carrots, peeled and cut in bite-size pieces
> 4 to 6 potatoes, peeled and cubed
> 1 T. Worcestershire Sauce
> 2 T. tapioca
> 1 T. sugar
> 1 T. salt
> Pepper to taste
> ½ C. water
> ½ C. red wine
> 1 large can crushed tomatoes

Preheat oven at 250°.

Place meat, vegetables, and seasonings into a Dutch oven.

Add tomatoes, water and wine.

Stir well.

Bake for five hours at 250°.

Don't peek!

Twice-Baked Potatoes and Potato Casserole

Marty has always made excellent Twice-Baked Potatoes. Recently, however, Jill's mother-in-law, Rita Brown, showed Marty how to turn the Twice-Baked Potato mixture into a lip-smacking casserole.

    4 medium russet potatoes, scrubbed and dried
    4 oz. cheddar cheese, shredded
    ½ C. sour cream
    ½ C. buttermilk
    2 T. unsalted butter, softened

Preheat oven at 450°.

Poke holes in each potato with a fork and microwave potatoes for 6 minutes.

Move unwrapped potatoes to hot oven (450°) and cook 20 to 30 minutes (until knife comes out smoothly).

Allow potatoes to cool for 10 minutes. Turn oven down to 350°.

Slice potatoes in halves. Scoop out flesh into a mixing bowl (leave about ¼-inch in the shell to provide structure).

Bake shells 10 minutes until crispy.

Mash potatoes until smooth. Stir in sour cream, buttermilk, butter, and half of the cheese. Season with salt and pepper to taste.

Spoon mixture into shells placed in a shallow baking dish. Top with the other half of cheese and bake for 15 to 20 minutes at 350°.

To make Twice-Baked Potato Casserole, double this recipe. Add 1 package of Ranch dressing mix to potato mixture and spread it into a 9x13 baking dish that has been sprayed generously with Pam. Top with other half of cheese and bake 20 minutes. Discard shells or use them to make Potato Skin Nachos.

Lime Jell-o Salad

This recipe has been around for a long time, but it is a refreshing side dish that goes with so many different entrees. It even makes leftovers taste good.

1 large can crushed pineapple
1 box of lime Jell-o
1 C. water
1 ctn. (8 oz.) cottage cheese
½ C. of pecans, chopped
1 ctn. of Cool Whip

Empty can of pineapple into a saucepan and heat.

Stir in dry Jell-o.

After Jell-o is dissolved, add water.

Add cottage cheese and pecans.

Allow to cool until slightly set.

Stir in Cool Whip until thoroughly mixed.

Pour into a 9x13 dish and chill until mixture is set.

Two Yummy Salad Dressings

The right salad dressing can turn an ordinary green salad into a delectable first course that will set the right tone for a memorable meal. The pink dressing comes from Marty's sister Sarah Maple. Marty has used it many times, and it always evokes requests for the recipe.

PINK DRESSING
1 C. vegetable oil
5 T. vinegar (preferably raspberry or red wine vinegar)
4 T. sour cream
1½ t. salt
½ t. dry mustard
2 T. sugar
2 cloves garlic
2 T. parsley

Process all ingredients except parsley until mixture is smooth.
Add parsley and mix a few seconds more.

BALSAMIC VINAIGRETTE
⅓ C. Balsamic Vinegar
1¼ T. olive oil
2 T. sugar
1 t. honey mustard
¼ t. salt
⅛ t. pepper

Pour ingredients into a jar and fasten lid.
Shake vigorously until ingredients are blended.

Chocolate Brownie Nut Muffins

This is a good way to serve chocolate cake to the family and keep the portion size relatively small–unless everyone decides to have two, which was often the case at our house.

2 sticks of butter
4 squares of semi-sweet chocolate
1¾ C. sugar
1 C. flour
4 eggs
Salt
1 t. vanilla
1 C. pecans or walnuts, chopped

Preheat oven at 325°.

Melt butter and chocolate in a saucepan.

Remove from heat and add sugar and flour.

Fold in eggs; add vanilla, a pinch of salt, and nuts.

Pour batter into muffin pans lined with muffin paper and bake 25 to 30 minutes at 325°. Do not over bake, as middle needs to be moist.

Remove from muffin pans and allow to cool on a rack.

OCC's First Lady

In 1972, local architect Richard Tredway designed a house to be used as the home for the Oklahoma Christian College president and his family. Avanelle Baird, wife of President James O. Baird, made many suggestions in planning the new home. She was especially sensitive to having a place where the president and his wife could entertain without it being disruptive to any children who were living at home. Adolph Warren built the house on Smiling Hill Boulevard, sited on the northwest quadrant of the campus, and the Bairds moved into the new residence in the summer of 1973.

When it became apparent that health concerns would compel James Baird to relinquish the presidency, the Bairds purchased their own building site on Benson Road. They designed a two-story home with a self-sufficient apartment on the second level and informed the Board of Trustees that they planned to vacate the newly constructed house on Smiling Hill Boulevard. Although they were encouraged to remain in the house owned by the College, the Bairds felt that it had been built for the purpose of entertaining campus guests and was best suited for the new president and his family. The Board conducted a nationwide search for a person to replace President Baird, and the outcome was that Baird's thirty-one-year-old protégé, J. Terry Johnson, was selected for the post.

Terry and Marty at Presidential Inauguration–September 1974

Now the Johnsons were in a dilemma. They had lived in their dream home in the woods for less than three years, yet the College's new house, designed especially for its president and his family, was only a year old and soon to be vacated. After spending some time in prayer, and shedding a few tears, the Johnsons placed the house on East Everett Road on the market. Beginning in September 1974, their new address became 2108 Smiling Hill Boulevard.

It's impossible to convey the complexity of emotions that consumed Marty upon Terry's accepting the Board's offer to become the

College's third president. The winds of transition came down upon the family like an Oklahoma tornado. Marty, who was only twenty-nine, was proud of her husband for the honor extended to him professionally; yet the girls, now six and four, were so young and needed both parents actively involved in their lives. The family had to move from their own home that was located away from the campus buzz into a house that belonged to someone else and was highly visible to all the traffic that motored up and down Smiling Hill Boulevard. Marty had some disquieting moments about the move and especially about the responsibilities and expectations others had of her and her family.

On top of those concerns, Terry was being asked to speak at a host of churches and civic clubs, travel to distant cities in search of funds for the College, and spend countless nights away from Marty and the girls to attend college-related functions on and off the campus. The strain on the young family was more than they had anticipated.

Marty was also being drawn into new roles of public service, often asked to fill speaking assignments that she felt ill-equipped to handle. She was being asked for favors by well-meaning friends with an expectation that the College's first lady would be amenable to almost any reasonable request. She took her turn as president of the Oklahoma Christian College Women's Association; she spoke often on OCC's Women's Day programs at the annual lectureship; she traveled throughout the College's primary trade area to speak at women's classes, forums, and retreats; and she accompanied Terry on some of his business trips and key-development calls.

It was not easy to keep any semblance of balance between private time with the family and the demands of Terry's new role. Even family vacations became fund-raising tours with a little sight-seeing thrown in to amuse the girls. As Avanelle Baird had warned Marty,

"The College will become Terry's mistress." And to some extent, it already had.

—

Now residing in the new house, the first couple lived under a campus-wide presumption that they would use the house to entertain college students, faculty and staff, trustees, alumni, and the many friends who visited campus. The front entry to the house should have been designed as a revolving door. On some occasions, Marty barely had time to put the house back in order before the next group was scheduled to show up for its event.

For many years in the early fall, the Johnsons hosted freshmen students for a hamburger cookout in the backyard. Almost every January, lectureship participants enjoyed a buffet in the president's home on Sunday night, immediately prior to the opening keynote address. The Japanese students who visited from Ibaraki Christian College were often entertained in the home. A Saturday breakfast was hosted each September as a means of welcoming all women who worked on campus, as well as the spouses of the men who were employed at the College. The list of home-entertaining events went on and on.

At first, Marty had very little outside help. Each event required hours of her time in preparation and sometimes even more hours and greater physical energy to clean up the mess. That began to change when Carrie Lou Little, a prominent resident of Ardmore, Oklahoma, and a long-time supporter of the OCC Women's Association, saw what was happening and took Marty under her angelic wing as a special project.

The turning point was a dinner prepared for the Ibaraki Christian students and their sponsors. Marty had decided to offer her guests fresh chicken crepes, hot off her new crepe pan. On top of that, dessert would be strawberry crepes, also using her newly acquired pan. Carrie Lou was at the dinner as a guest, but before the night was over, she was in the kitchen with sleeves rolled up, helping Marty prepare hundreds of homemade crepes. The night was a fiasco.

Marty entertains Ibaraki Christian College students in her home

Fortified by Carrie Lou's insistence and clout, Terry sought the Board's approval to secure domestic help at the president's house and catering assistance from the College's food service staff. Marty never asked for, nor did she ever receive any compensation from the College for her hospitality role, but after this turning point, she was able to expect more assistance from the College to help her entertain campus guests.

Over the years, that service improved and became a critical factor in allowing the Johnsons to entertain as extensively as they did. Kattie Perry, a gentle woman who had years of experience in cleaning homes and preparing meals, became an extended part of the Johnson family–cleaning, washing, and helping with innumerable catering functions. With Kattie in the kitchen, Marty found it easier to relax and play the role of hostess at special events held in her home.

Kurt Hermanson became Marty's "go-to guy" at the College's food service program on campus. They shared recipes and often worked together as a team. Kurt was a bright, resourceful, and dependable colleague. Marty still spent long hours preparing for events that were hosted in her home, but execution and cleanup became more manageable than before.

Kattie Perry–a family friend and an integral part of Marty's hospitality team

Beef Stroganoff

Although introduced to Stroganoff while in Dallas, Marty developed her own skills with the recipe after moving to Oklahoma City. A good green salad, Stroganoff, and homemade bread made a hearty meal for our family or for guests.

 1½ lb. sirloin steak, cut into 1" strips
 Flour
 1½ t. salt
 2 onions, finely chopped
 ½ lb. mushrooms, chopped
 1 clove garlic, minced
 6 T. butter
 1 can (10½ oz.) beef broth
 1 pint sour cream
 1 t. paprika
 1 T. Worcestershire sauce

Dredge steak in flour, seasoning with salt and pepper.

Melt butter in a large skillet and sauté onions, mushrooms, and garlic for 5 minutes.

Add steak and cook over high heat for 3 minutes, stirring constantly. Remove steak and vegetables from skillet, saving the drippings.

Blend 2 tablespoons flour with 2 tablespoons of the drippings in the skillet. Add broth and stir until smooth and thickened.

Add steak and vegetables to broth, cover, and place over low heat for 30 minutes.

Stir in sour cream, paprika, and Worcestershire sauce, bringing mixture back to a boil.

Serve over white rice.

Crepes–Chicken and Strawberry

You may wish to purchase a crepe pan before tackling these recipes, and, from Marty's experience, you may not want to serve both at the same meal.

CREPES
2 eggs
2 T. butter, melted
1½ C. milk
1 C. flour
½ t. salt
1 T. sugar

Place ingredients in a blender in given order.

Blend on high speed for 30 seconds.

Scrape sides of blender and blend again for 20 seconds.

The batter may be refrigerated at this time or used immediately.

When ready to use, put 2 or 3 tablespoons of batter into a medium-sized warm, slightly greased crepe pan (or a 6- to 7-inch skillet). Tilt pan to spread batter, making a thin crepe.

When crepe is lightly browned, flip over and cook other side.

CHICKEN FILLING
2 T. butter
1 T. onion or shallots, minced
2 T. flour
1½ C. half 'n half milk
1 C. cooked chicken, diced
¼ C. sherry

¼ C. grated parmesan cheese
¼ C. sliced almonds

In a saucepan, melt butter; add shallots and sauté until yellow.

Add flour and cook until bubbly.

Add half 'n half and cook until thick and smooth.

Set aside half of the sauce for later use.

Add chicken and sherry to half of the sauce.

Place 2 tablespoons of chicken filling into a crepe and roll.

Place crepes into a buttered shallow casserole dish.

Cover with remaining sauce.

Sprinkle with cheese and sliced almonds.

Bake at 450° until brown.

STRAWBERRY FILLING
1 qt. of fresh strawberries, sliced, sprin-
kled with sugar, and allowed to sit
for several hours before using
16 oz. cream cheese, softened
⅓ C. sugar
1 t. almond extract
2 C. sour cream
Cool Whip

Use an electric mixer to blend cream cheese with sugar and almond extract.

Mix in sour cream, blending well.

Makes 4½ cups of filling.

Spoon into warm crepes and top with sliced strawberries and whipped cream.

Chicken Parmesan

This entrée is a winner, and it will make a winner out of you with the whole family. If the ingredients are on hand, you can prepare dinner in a matter of minutes.

6 boneless, skinless chicken breasts
2 T. butter, melted
½ C. grated parmesan cheese
¼ C. dry bread crumbs
1 t. dried oregano
1 t. parsley flakes
¼ t. paprika
¼ t. garlic powder
¼ t. salt
¼ t. pepper

Lightly grease a 9x13 baking dish.

Preheat oven at 400°.

Dip chicken in butter.

Mix all other dry ingredients in a bowl.

Coat chicken with dry mixture ingredients.

Place coated chicken in baking dish.

Bake 20 to 25 minutes at 400° until pink is gone in thickest part of chicken.

Lemon Chess Pie

This was my favorite pie for many years. Marty quit baking it because she said my waistline couldn't take it anymore. Tacky. Tacky.

½ C. butter
1½ C. sugar
2 T. flour
2 T. corn meal
¾ C. whole milk
1 t. vanilla
Juice of ½ to 1 lemon according to taste
4 eggs
Dash of salt

Preheat oven to 325°.

Cream butter.

Mix sugar, flour, and corn meal and add to butter, blending well.

Beat eggs well and fold into sugar mixture.

Blend milk into mixture, pouring small amounts in at a time.

Add lemon juice, vanilla, and salt.

Pour into a partially-baked pie crust shell and bake for 30 minutes at 325°. Pie is done when middle has no jiggle.

Butter Pecan Turtle Bars

Marty made hundreds of Hello Dollies while living in Oklahoma City. The college students loved them and Dollies were relatively easy to make. But they are so 1970ish. Here is a 21st-century upgrade, with special thanks to Marty's sister-in-law, Vickie Mitchell.

2 C. flour
¾ C. packed light brown sugar
½ C. butter, softened
1½ C. pecan halves
½ C. light brown sugar
⅔ C. butter
1½ C. milk chocolate chips

Preheat oven at 350°.

Combine flour, ¾ cup brown sugar, and ½ cup softened butter. Blend until crumbly.

Pat firmly onto bottom of ungreased 9x13 baking dish.

Sprinkle pecans over unbaked crust and set aside.

Combine ½ cup brown sugar and ⅔ cup butter in a saucepan. Cook over medium heat, stirring constantly, until mixture begins to boil. Boil for 1 minute, constantly stirring.

Drizzle caramel mixture over pecans and crust.

Bake for 18 to 20 minutes at 350°.

Remove from oven and sprinkle chocolate chips over uncut bars.

Cool completely before cutting into 48 bars.

Marty and Mable at Thanksgiving
The Edmond Sun
–November 24, 1988

The Green Herb

In the fall of 1976, Jill began first grade at Chisholm Elementary School in Edmond. Jennifer was a third-grader at the same school. For the first time in eight years, Marty found some breathing room in her daytime schedule. There were always luncheons and fund raisers with OCCWA, ladies classes at church, and a tennis match or two to fill part of each day; but she struggled to find a creative outlet for her own unique talents—something that was her own individual undertaking.

One morning, Marty and her mother were lamenting the fact that there were not many places where they could purchase natural foods that were untainted with pesticides and other harsh chemicals. Mable, an artist, was always looking for a place to show her paintings. She suggested that the two of them start their own health food store to sell juices, yogurts, whole-grain cereals, vitamins, and other related products. Mable would decorate the store walls with her paintings.

A convenience grocery store operated in a small shopping center at the corner of Benson and Memorial Roads. Because the grocery was unable to use the entire 3600-square-foot space, approximately 1000 square feet in the rear of the store was available to sub-let. Marty and Mable liked the location, so they secured a small line-of-credit loan from First National Bank in Edmond and opened The Green Herb.

In many respects, The Green Herb was a cry 'from Marty for her own space and for her own identity. Operating her own business was a distraction from the heavy demands on her time, whether real or imagined, that she felt from the campus community. She was proud of Terry and the activities that centered round the College, but it was not a role she had cast for herself. At the College, she was an appendage of the president's office; at The Green Herb, she was owner and operator.

Marty cutting fresh vegetables at The Green Herb. Photo and article appeared in The Sunday Oklahoman –April 1977

The new store developed a nice clientele but was never the overwhelming success Marty and Mable had hoped it would become. Keeping store hours six days a week was confining for the two women, who had been used to having greater flexibility in their daily schedules. After a year, the lease was up, and the entrepreneurs decided not to renew it.

Another factor that contributed to Marty's decision to close The Green Herb was an unexpected addition to the Johnson family. Terry's niece, five-year-old Tiffanie Johnson from Springfield, needed a stable home. The child of a broken marriage, Tiffanie had been living with Terry's parents, who were finding it difficult to keep up with the many needs of their pre-school granddaughter. Marty insisted that Tiffanie move to Edmond and live with her cousins. In 1978, Tiffanie began kindergarten in the Edmond Public Schools.

Tiffanie–circa 1978

—

Carrie Lou Little continued to be a source of great encouragement to Marty. She was both a mentor and a confidant. Whenever possible, Marty took the three girls to Ardmore, where she shopped for their school clothes at The Daube, a fashionable department store that was owned by Carrie Lou's good friend, Olive Daube. After a day of shopping, Carrie Lou would entertain her guests with some aquatic recreation, swimming and boating at nearby Lake Murray.

The hospitality was reciprocal. Carrie Lou's husband, Quintin Little, a prominent oilman in Ardmore, was in very poor health, requiring 24-hour nursing care. Carrie Lou found Marty's youthful enthusiasm good tonic at a time when she herself was under considerable stress as a caregiver. Carrie Lou came to many campus events during these years, pouring herself into the mission of Oklahoma Christian College. After a few years of intensive involvement with the College, she agreed to serve as the first woman on its Board of Trustees.

For three consecutive years, the Johnsons invited Carrie Lou to accompany them to New York City when the U. S. Tennis Open was being held at Forest Hills. While Terry made corporate and foundation calls during the day, the ladies shopped Fifth Avenue and a few small boutiques known only to Carrie Lou. In the evenings, Terry would join the ladies for dinner and the theatre or tennis matches in Queens.

Among her more sterling qualities, Carrie Lou loved to be with young people. She regularly picked up teenagers in her van and brought them to the Maxwell Avenue Church of Christ on Sundays and on Wednesday nights. Dozens of students attended Harding College or Oklahoma Christian College because Carrie Lou paid their tuition and fees. She found a number of at-risk students and made whatever provisions were needed to stabilize their lives.

Carrie Lou Little, Marty and Faye Hogan at an Oklahoma Christian dinner party

One of Carrie Lou's "projects" was a young lady named Deborah Roy. Debbie was a beautiful girl who had grown up in a difficult home environment. Carrie Lou was hopeful that she could make a difference in Debbie's life.

One day, Carrie Lou called Marty and asked if there was any way Debbie could live with the Johnsons and attend Living Word Academy, the Christian school in Oklahoma City. Jennifer was now attending LWA. Although all of her bedrooms were filled, Marty set up a room for Debbie in the small study off the foyer and she lived with the Johnsons for one school year. Marty would do anything for her friend Carrie Lou.

—

Still trying to find a creative outlet for her own personal skill-sets, Marty applied for an editing job with The Economy Company, a book publisher that was headquartered in Oklahoma City. The position was an eight-to-five workday, five days a week. The starting salary was minimal, but Marty had the satisfaction of bringing home her own paycheck and contributing to the financial needs of her growing family. Terry had not taken any outside legal cases since he became president, and the salaries paid at the College were relatively small, even for their top-tiered administrators.

Once again, however, the grind of spending forty hours each week outside the home, while still handling the many duties associated with being the College's first lady, created a conflict that was not working at home. Marty felt handcuffed by the schedule and guilty for missing so many campus and family events. She left The Economy Company after a year and focused her attention on raising her girls, who needed a full-time mom. Every afternoon at 3:00, Marty retired to her bedroom, turned off the lights, and listened to Dr. James Dobson's radio program, *Focus on the Family*. It was the therapy she needed to keep all of plates in her life spinning at the same time.

Herb-Marinated Roasted Turkey Breast

It doesn't have to be Thanksgiving to enjoy this meal. The leftovers are the best to be found in the refrigerator.

4 to 6 lb. turkey breast

MARINADE:
¼ C. olive oil
¼ C. white wine vinegar
2 t. rosemary, crushed
1 t. sage
1 t. salt
½ t. coarsely ground black pepper
2 cloves garlic, minced

GRAVY
1½ C. chicken broth
2 T. cornstarch
¼ C. white wine
¼ C. heavy cream

Place turkey breast in large zip-lock bag.

Blend marinade ingredients and add to the turkey bag; press out air and seal; coat turkey with the marinade; refrigerate marinated turkey in the bag for several hours or overnight.

The next day, preheat oven at 325°.

Remove turkey from bag and place on a rack in an open pan, spreading herbs and garlic from marinade all over the turkey. Discard remainder of marinade.

Roast 1¾ to 2½ hours or until meat thermometer reaches 175°. Remove turkey and keep warm.

Turkey Gravy

Combine ½ cup of chicken broth with cornstarch in the roasting pan. Add remaining chicken broth, scraping up the pan's juices.

Pour into a saucepan, adding wine, and bring to a boil.

Add cream and cornstarch. Cook until thickened and clear.

Cornbread Dressing

What's roasted turkey without dressing? Marty began using her mother's recipe for dressing, but it was extra heavy on the giblets. Over time, she developed her own cornbread dressing that has won rave reviews at many holiday meals.

3 C. onions, finely chopped
1½ C. celery, finely chopped
1 stick unsalted butter
1½ lbs. bulk pork sausage
2 C. half 'n half
12 C. cornbread, cut in 1" pieces and dried on
cookie sheets in the oven at 250° for 45 minutes
3 C. of broth from turkey, or use chicken broth
2 large eggs, beaten lightly
2 T. fresh thyme leaves, minced
2 T. fresh sage leaves, minced
3 garlic cloves, minced
1 t. salt
2 t. ground black pepper

Place dried cornbread in a large bowl.

In a medium bowl, whisk stock, half 'n half, and eggs; pour over cornbread and toss gently so that cornbread does not break into small pieces; set aside.

Heat large, heavy skillet over medium-high heat for 1 minute; add 2 tablespoons butter to coat bottom of skillet; add sausage and cook for 5 to 7 minutes; with slotted spoon, remove sausage into a medium bowl.

Add half of onions and celery to the fat left in the skillet; sauté for 5 minutes, stirring as needed to keep from burning; transfer onion mixture to the bowl with the sausage.

Melt 6 tablespoons butter in the skillet; add remaining onion and celery and sauté 5 minutes, stirring occasionally; stir in thyme, sage, and garlic and cook for 30 seconds; add salt and pepper.

Add this mixture to sausage and onion mixture and pour over cornbread, stirring gently to combine without breaking cornbread into smaller pieces.

Cover bowl with plastic wrap and refrigerate 1 to 4 hours to blend flavors.

Adjust oven rack to lower-middle position and heat oven to 400°.

Butter a 10x15 baking dish (or two 9x9) and pour stuffing mixture into dish; bake 35 to 40 minutes, until golden brown.

Cranberry Jell-o Salad

Until she found this recipe, Marty made a similar salad with straw-berries. Either one is an attractive and delicious dish at the holidays, but this one is slightly firmer and has become a family favorite.

1 lb. fresh cranberries
1 C. sugar
1 pkg. (3 oz.) cranberry Jell-o
1 C. boiling water
1 can (20 oz.) crushed pineapple, drained
1½ C. pecans, chopped
1 C. mini marshmallows
½ pint whipping cream, whipped (or 8 oz. Cool Whip)

Rinse and chop cranberries in food processor until finely chopped.

Mix cranberries with sugar and allow to sit several hours (or overnight).

Dissolve Jell-o in boiling water.

Add cranberries and remaining ingredients, folding in whipped cream last.

Place in large glass bowl and chill until firm.

Morning Glory Muffins

Marty discovered this recipe when she was operating her health food store, The Green Herb. These muffins replaced the family's former breakfast diet of Ding Dongs and Hostess Cupcakes.

½ C. raisins, plumped in brandy
  or apple juice and drained
2 C. all-purpose flour
1 C. sugar
2 t. baking soda
2 t. cinnamon
½ t. salt
2 C. carrots, peeled and grated
1 large tart green apple, peeled, cored, and grated
½ C. pecans, chopped
½ C. coconut, shredded
3 eggs
1 C. vegetable oil
2 t. vanilla

Preheat oven at 375°.

Spray Pam in muffin tins.

Mix flour, sugar, soda, cinnamon, and salt in a bowl.

Stir in raisins, apple, carrots, pecans, and coconut.

Beat eggs with oil and vanilla to blend; stir into flour mixture until barely combined.

Place ½ cup of the mixture into each muffin tin.

Bake at 375° for 20 minutes. Serve at room temperature.

Granola Supreme

Although The Green Herb was not a rousing financial success, it did bring some healthy changes to the family's diet. Marty learned about whole grains and nutrition from her exposure to the health food industry. It was a good stepping stone for her later success as a marketing executive with an international health and wellness company.

     3 C. old-fashioned rolled oats
     1½ C. raw pistachios, hulled
     1 C. raw pumpkin seeds, hulled
     1 C. coconut flakes
     ¾ C. maple syrup
     ½ C. extra virgin olive oil
     ½ C. packed light brown sugar
     1 t. kosher salt
     ½ t. cinnamon
     ½ t. ground cardamom
     ¾ C. dried apricots, chopped

Preheat oven at 300°.

Use a large mixing bowl to combine oats, pistachios, pumpkin seeds, coconut, syrup, olive oil, brown sugar, salt, cinnamon, and cardamom.

Spread mixture evenly on a rimmed baking sheet and bake for 45 minutes, stirring every 10 minutes until golden brown and well toasted.

Transfer granola to a large bowl and add apricots, mixing thoroughly.

Peanut Butter Cookies

Nothing warmed the hearts and opened the pocketbooks of OCC's major donors quicker than those occasions when Marty baked them a dozen of her scrumptious Peanut Butter Cookies.

½ C. dark brown sugar
½ C. white sugar
1 stick butter
1 egg
1 C. smooth peanut butter
½ t. salt
½ t. soda
1½ C. of sifted flour
½ t. vanilla

Grease one or two cookie sheets.

Preheat oven at 350°.

Cream both sugars with butter.

Beat in egg, peanut butter, salt, and soda.

Blend in flour.

Add vanilla.

Roll dough into ping-pong-sized balls and place on a greased cookie sheet.

Flatten dough with a fork.

Bake 12 to 15 minutes at 350°, or until slightly brown on the edges.

High Society

If all the entertaining in the OCC president's home had been charcoaled hamburgers for students and faculty and endless buffets for alumni and church-member friends, it would have been undeniably worthwhile. But, in fact, it was much more than that. Some of the most successful business leaders in Oklahoma and from across the United States sat at Marty's table, dining on ratatouille and broiled beef tenderloin, cooked to perfection, and raving over her lemon chess pie. She had become an excellent cook.

Marty had the gift of making company feel welcomed and relaxed in her home, charming them with animated stories about the family and with poignant passages from her favorite authors. It were as if for a couple of hours, these invited guests were under her magical spell.

Marty hosts guests in the Oklahoma Christian President's Dining Room

That's not to say that every event went exactly according to plan. On one occasion the Johnsons were hosting John and Eleanor Kirkpatrick for dinner. The Kirkpatricks were among the most influential families in Oklahoma City and known for making generous gifts to many charitable and non-profit organizations. Aware that the Kirkpatricks especially loved music and the fine arts, Terry had invited them to dinner and a performance on campus by the internationally acclaimed soprano, Roberta Peters, who was appearing as part of the College's arts festival known as Gala Week. Preparation for the dinner had been underway for days.

Early on the morning of the highly anticipated event, Terry and Marty were awakened by the sharp barking of their family's new pet, an Australian Silky Terrier named Betsy. The dog slept under their bed and usually needed to be let outside each morning through a sliding patio door. Being awakened by shrill barking was not part of the daily routine.

Hearing Betsy's fierce yapping, Terry lunged out of bed, ready to let the dog out through the sliding patio door. Feeling the cool, refreshing night air pouring into the bedroom through the screened door, he realized that the barking was not coming from the bedroom, but from the backyard. He had apparently already let Betsy outside; he now needed to let her back in.

As he reached for the sliding door's handle to pull back the screen and allow Betsy to come back into the house, Terry suddenly recognized that the shadow outside the screened door was not Betsy–she was out in the backyard barking her head off. Panic-stricken, he slammed the patio glass door shut, but he was a few seconds too late. The entire house had been gassed by a skunk that had been penned up against the bedroom's screened door by the menacing dog in the Johnsons' backyard.

Jerry Adams, a local news anchor, and a personal friend of the Johnsons, heard of the incident and had some fun with it on the noon news report. Someone called Adams and told him to have the Johnsons use eucalyptus oil to get rid of the smell. A dozen bowls filled with the liquid were spread throughout the house that afternoon, and when it was time for dinner, the Kirkpatricks were entertained as if nothing unusual had happened that day. Only Betsy missed the dinner. She was left overnight at the groomers for a trim and extra shampooing.

—

Marty became interested in needle-point stitching as a hobby. She took some lessons and tried her hand at beginner patterned pillows, discovering that she truly enjoyed the craft. In time, she became very proficient in her skills, making a variety of intricate pieces from pillows to wall hangings to Christmas tree ornaments. For five years, she needle-pointed ornaments and gave them to some of the College's largest donors at Christmas. The women who received the needle-work treasured them as special gifts and knew that each one had taken hours of Marty's time.

One person who was especially impressed with Marty's needle-point was Thelma Gaylord, the spouse of Oklahoma's most influential businessman, Edward L. Gaylord. The Gaylords had been good friends of the College ever since it moved from Bartlesville to Oklahoma City in 1958. Mr. Gaylord had led several funding campaigns for Dr. Baird and later for Terry when he became president. But Mrs. Gaylord stayed more in the shadows, preferring to allow her husband to keep ties with the College rather than doing so herself—until she met Marty. Their friendship began slowly, but it grew into a genuine love for one another that flourished as the years passed by.

The Gaylords were frequent guests in the Johnsons' home and vice versa. More often, they met each other for dinner at Sleepy Hollow or Hunan's, sharing stories about their families and political events of the day. Marty delighted in making Ed and Thelma laugh. As Terry watched his wife amuse her guests at a dinner table, he was fond of saying, "Marty is my social crutch."

Occasionally, Marty and Thelma went on shopping sprees to Dallas or to Ardmore where they would lunch with Carrie Lou and then visit the local dress shops. The Jean Lee was a boutique in Ardmore that attracted well-heeled shoppers from throughout Oklahoma and North Texas. It offered the latest fashion from all the top designers—from Dior and Oscar de la Renta to Versace and Armani. The store was often equated with the exclusive shops in New York City. Thelma loved her trips with Marty, always feeling that she was with someone she could trust as a true friend.

As the years passed, the friendship between the Gaylords and the Johnsons grew into something much deeper than "a college president and his major donor." The couples truly cared for one another. The Gaylords always included the Johnsons in the social activities associated with their family's privately owned company– The Oklahoma Publishing Company. They flew the Johnsons and other friends from Oklahoma City to Nashville to celebrate Gaylord Entertainment's fifth year of ownership of The Grand Ole Opry and related properties. They did the same when it was time to showcase a major renovation to the family's prize purchase in Colorado Springs, the exquisite Broadmoor Hotel.

Marty pins a corsage on Thelma Gaylord, co-honoree with husband Edward L. Gaylord at Oklahoma Christian College's annual Spring Dinner

Of all the events hosted by Marty in her home, two small luncheons stand out as being especially memorable. The first was in 1982 when Enterprise Square, USA, was opened to the public. Some of the major donors, including Olive Garvey, the matriarch of Wichita, Kansas; Stanley and Dorothy Kresge, third generation of the Michigan family responsible for the K-Mart Stores; Ed and Thelma Gaylord; Phillips Petroleum Chairman William F. Martin and his wife, Betty; and local attorney Robert Reese and his mother,

Eleanor Hamill, joined the Johnsons in a pre-celebratory meal at the president's house. Terry and his staff may have raised the contributions to build the new economic center, but the friendships with these donors were solidified around a meal of luncheon-sized beef filets and twice-baked potatoes prepared by Marty.

The second luncheon, five years later, was a similar event–this time to honor Sam and Helen Walton, founders of the internationally acclaimed Wal-Mart and Sam's Stores. That same evening Mr. Walton received Enterprise Square's newly inaugurated Libertas Award at a black-tie dinner at the Oklahoma City Marriott.

The Gaylords attended the luncheon, along with Carrie Lou and her husband, Robert H. Davis, Jr.–the same Dallas attorney that had hired Terry fifteen years earlier at Otis Engineering. After Quintin Little's death, the Johnsons had introduced Carrie Lou to Bob, a widower, and they had married six months later. This time, in honor of the folksy image Mr. Walton had established for himself, Marty prepared skillet-fried chicken breasts and six side dishes made from the fresh vegetables Marty had picked from her mother's garden. Throughout the luncheon, she matched Sam Walton story for story and had him begging for more.

Broiled Beef Tenderloin

Beef tenderloin was often the entrée of choice for small dinner parties in the Oklahoma Christian president's house. Green salad, twice-baked potatoes, hot rolls, and a dessert comprised a winning ticket every time.

> 1 trimmed beef tenderloin (3½ to 3¾ lb.)
> 2 T. vegetable oil
> Salt
> Pepper

Preheat oven at 425°, placing rack in upper-middle position.

Pat tenderloin dry; brush with vegetable oil.

Rub pepper over tenderloin and sprinkle with salt.

Place tenderloin on a rack in a shallow roasting pan and roast for 15 minutes at 425°.

Reduce oven temperature to 350° and roast for 25 minutes for medium (30 minutes max).

Transfer tenderloin to a cutting board, tenting meat with foil. Allow to stand for 15 minutes before carving so that juices will not escape. Slice ½-inch thick and serve with horseradish sauce or mushroom gravy.

Mustard Horseradish Cream Sauce

Whisk together ⅓ cup Dijon mustard, ⅓ cup sour cream, ¼ cup mayonnaise, and ¼ cup well-drained prepared white horseradish. Refrigerate until ready to use.

Mushroom Gravy

1 T. vegetable oil
2 shallots, minced
8 oz. white button mushrooms, sliced thin
¼ C. dry sherry or white wine
1 C. heavy cream
½ C. chicken broth

Heat vegetable oil in skillet on medium-high setting.

Add shallots and salt; cook for 2 minutes.

Add mushrooms; cook until brown (8 minutes).

Add sherry or wine and cook for 1 minute.

Stir in cream and broth and simmer until thickened (8 minutes).

Salt and pepper to taste.

Ratatouille

Occasionally, Marty invited a local chef to prepare dinner for her guests. Chef John taught her how to make Ratatouille, which was just about as French as the cuisine got at the president's house.

2 lbs. zucchini
2 lbs. eggplant, peeled
⅓ C. butter
3 green peppers, sliced thin
2 onions, sliced
3 cloves garlic
2 lbs. tomatoes
Salt and pepper
Basil, thyme, and bay leaf

Preheat oven at 350°.

Cut unpeeled zucchini and peeled eggplant into ½-inch slices and sauté in a skillet, using the butter, only a few vegetables at a time, and sautéing several minutes on each side. Remove and drain.

Cook green peppers, onions, and garlic in same skillet for 10 minutes. Remove and discard garlic.

Peel, seed, and slice tomatoes; add to peppers and onions in skillet.

In a baking dish, layer eggplant, zucchini, and half the tomato mixture; season with salt, pepper, and herbs; repeat layering with remaining vegetables, ending with tomato sauce and seasonings. Bake covered for about 1 hour at 350°.

Baked Curried Fruit

This is another recipe that was often seen at one of Marty's brunches or luncheons. It always made the house smell so good when guests arrived.

1 can (16 oz.) pear halves, quartered, drained
1 can (16 oz.) pineapple chunks,
drained, (reserve ½ C. juice)
1 can (16 oz.) apricot halves, drained
1 can (16 oz.) sliced peaches, drained
1 can (16 oz.) dark Bing cherries, drained
½ C. brown sugar
¼ t. curry powder
½ t. salt
1 t. cinnamon
2 T. cornstarch
½ C. butter

Drain canned fruit, mix thoroughly, and place evenly in a lightly buttered 9x13 baking dish.

Mix reserved ½ cup pineapple juice with butter in a saucepan and heat until butter is melted.

Mix dry ingredients in a bowl and stir into butter mixture until well combined.

Pour the sugar mixture evenly over the fruit.

Bake uncovered 40 minutes at 375°.

Allow to sit 15 minutes before serving.

Manhattan Cheesecake

Some hostesses serve this cheesecake with a fruit topping, but Marty has always thought it was better without anything detracting from the pure flavor of the cake itself.

CRUST
7½ oz. Vanilla Wafer crumbs, crushed fine
1 C. pecan pieces
1 stick butter, melted

Preheat oven at 325°.

Stir ingredients until mixed well.

Pat mixture into the bottom of a 10-inch spring-form pan.

FILLING
24 oz. cream cheese
1½ C. sugar
4 eggs
½ t. almond extract

Mix ingredients together, adding one egg at a time.

Pour mixture into crust and bake for one hour at 325°.

TOPPING
1 pt. sour cream
1½ C. sugar
½ t. vanilla

Mix ingredients in a bowl with a spoon.

Pour topping on cheesecake and bake 10 to 15 minutes longer.

Allow to cool at room temperature before serving or before placing into refrigerator.

Apple Pie with Rum Sauce

Marty hosted many women's luncheons at Alberta's Tea Room in Oklahoma City and became acquainted with Larry, the restaurant's celebrated chef. He catered a few parties at the president's house, always bringing his apple pie with rum sauce as the dessert.

CRUST
2 C. flour
¾ C. Crisco
½ C. cold water
1 t. salt

Cut the Crisco into the flour until it forms small nuggets.

Mix salt with cold water and add to flour mixture.

Roll dough until it becomes smooth, but do not over handle.

Line 9"-pie pan bottom and sides with part of the dough, approximately ¼-inch thick and save the rest for the top crust.

FILLING
4 to 6 tart apples (approximately 5 cups, using a variety of apples - Winesaps, Granny Smiths, McIntoshes)
2 T. flour
1 tsp cinnamon
⅔ C. sugar
½ t. nutmeg
1 t. vanilla
Salt
2 T. butter, cut into small pieces

Preheat oven at 400°.

Peel, core, and slice apples.

Fill bottom of uncooked pie shell with sliced apples.

Mix flour, sugar, vanilla, cinnamon, nutmeg, and pinch of salt in a bowl. Pour over apples.

Place butter pieces on top and wet edges of bottom crust with water.

Cover with top crust and press edges of two crusts together, making ridges with your thumb.

Brush top crust with water and sprinkle with sugar.

Bake for 45 to 50 minutes at 400°.

RUM SAUCE
½ C. heavy cream
½ stick unsalted butter at room temperature
½ C. sugar
2 egg yolks, lightly beaten
2 T. rum

Use a small, heavy saucepan to bring cream to a boil.

Stir in butter and sugar.

Whisk in egg yolks, stirring constantly until mixture thickens. Do not boil.

Remove from heat and stir in rum.

When pie is removed from oven, brush on rum sauce, more or less to taste.

Carrie Lou's Chocolate Pie

This old recipe was a favorite of Carrie Lou Little Davis, Marty's good friend from Ardmore. Carrie Lou always set an exquisite dining table to entertain her guests.

    1 C. sugar
    5 T. all-purpose flour
    ½ t. salt
    ¼ C. cocoa powder
    2 C. milk
    4 egg yolks, slightly beaten (save
        whites for meringue)
    3 T. unsalted butter
    1½ t. vanilla extract

....

Preheat oven at 350°.

Mix sugar, flour, cocoa, egg yolks, and salt into a saucepan.

Slowly stir in milk and cook at medium-high heat until mixture becomes thick and boils; boil for 1 minute.

Remove from heat and stir in butter and vanilla.

Transfer mixture to a bowl; cover pudding surface with plastic wrap and allow to cool.

Pour into baked pie shell and top with meringue.

MERINGUE
    5 egg whites
    ½ C. sugar
    1 t. vanilla
    ½ t. cream of tartar
    Salt

....

Beat egg whites, a pinch of salt, and cream of tartar in a stainless steel bowl until foamy; add sugar, 1 tablespoon at a time.

Beat to stiff peaks; add vanilla and beat to stiff peaks.

Pour over pie, making sure meringue touches edges of crust and bake for 10 minutes at 350°.

International
Tour Hostess

When the Johnsons returned from a holiday trip to Hawaii with the men's basketball team in 1980, Terry began to consider the possibilities of the College's hosting alumni, trustees, and key donors on an annual excursion to various international destinations. The first of these tours was a Caribbean cruise that was scheduled for the spring of 1982. Sixty adventurous travelers signed up for the trip.

Among those travelling with the Johnsons were co-hosts Guy and Mary Ann Ross; four trustees and their spouses; Terry's and Marty's parents; and Bible chairman Raymond Kelcy and his wife, Hester. Since the ship was at sea on Sunday, the group held worship services in one of the spacious lounges. Dr. Kelcy, who had been asked to preach, stood in front of the expansive bar with his Bible held wide open. Liquor bottles could be seen on the shelves behind him. He began his remarks by asking, "Would someone please take a picture of me in front of this bar? I want to send it to *The Gospel Advocate.*"

Raymond Kelcy anticipates a large piece of cake as he and others celebrate Mable Mitchell's birthday on the 1982 Caribbean cruise.

The entire week was a delightful experience. Everyone enjoyed the port stops, the food, and the ship-board entertainment. It was the first time many of the guests had been on a cruise ship.

As with any large group, however, there were a few travelers who were experiencing small problems along the way. One was Teady Mann, the tour guide assigned by the travel agency to accompany the OCC party. Teady had agreed to be the roommate of an elderly lady (let's call her *Helen*, which was not her real name). From all appearances, Helen was struggling with some form of dementia.

Marty was concerned that Teady was being worn down by Helen's erratic behavior. On Thursday at lunch, Marty told Teady that she would be glad to stay with Helen that night and that Teady could sleep in Marty and Terry's stateroom. It was a kind gesture, typical of Marty's concern for others, but it left Terry without a bed for the night.

A man without a stateroom, Terry decided that he would pass the night watching movies at the theater or reading a book in some lounge chair until he fell asleep. Shortly after midnight, Marty sent a steward to find Terry in the movie theater and have him come to Helen's stateroom, where she and Helen were spending the night.

Once Terry arrived, Marty convinced him that the two of them could sleep in the single bed if they lay side-by-side like spoons. They decided to give it a try. It worked fairly well until Marty needed to get up and visit the restroom. The stirring around woke Helen, who sat up in her bed, looked at the other bed across the room, and exclaimed, "Why, Terry Johnson! What are you doing in my room?" The story of the president's inexplicable presence in an elderly lady's stateroom during early-morning hours was retold many times on campus to the delight of amused faculty and friends.

The Caribbean cruise was the first of many international tours hosted by the Johnsons and the Rosses on behalf of the College. Through these shared experiences, friends of the College became stronger in their allegiance to Oklahoma Christian. Each trip was an enjoyable adventure, but Marty was always mindful of the responsibility she and Terry felt to ensure every traveler's safety and good feelings about the journey. The tour, after all, was about building goodwill for the College.

Mary Ann Ross and Marty, co-hosts of many international trips, examine the unusual flora on one of the Caribbean Islands.

—

The Johnsons' two daughters, Jennifer and Jill, two years apart, gave their parents very little grief during their teenage years and had soon blossomed into two kind and caring young ladies. After living in Oklahoma five years, Tiffanie had moved back to Springfield to live with her father and her new step-mother, and Debbie Roy had only stayed with the Johnsons one year before returning to Ardmore.

When Jennifer turned sixteen, she went on the College's first tour to Israel and roomed with Terry's mother. Jill went on a similar tour for her sixteenth birthday–this time another Caribbean cruise. Millie Prince, a young widow who later married Bobby Roberson and became an OCC trustee, providing major funding for the new engineering program, was Jill's roommate.

As high school graduation approached, Jennifer gave serious consideration to attending Harding University. She had Marty's blessings but knew that her dad would be disappointed if she chose not to attend Oklahoma Christian. Jill had a similar experience when she was making her college choice, only in her case the other school was Abilene Christian University. Again, she had her mother's support, but in the end, the daughters chose to attend Oklahoma Christian College. Both girls participated in the newly established Vienna Studies Program and thought it was the highlight of their college careers.

Jennifer married Royce L. Clark in March 1989. Royce was an engineering major from New Mexico and had worked part-time at Enterprise Square, USA, as a tour guide and assistant technician. Jennifer had also worked in the offices of Enterprise Square, USA. Not surprisingly, their wedding reception was held in the Hall of Giants and in other exhibit rooms throughout the building.

Over the years, Jill has been teased that her wedding was arranged by her mother and mother-in-law. One weekend in early September 1989, Terry and Marty traveled to Midland, Texas, where Terry had been asked to preach at the Golf Course Road Church of Christ. The Johnsons were being hosted by Jack and Wanda McGraw and Dale and Rita Brown.

During dinner, Rita and Marty began visiting about their unmarried children. Jill was in Vienna. The Browns' son, Cary, had recently graduated from Abilene Christian and had taken a job in Houston. Rita called Marty a week later to get Jill's address in Vienna. Cary sent Jill a letter, and the romance was on. They married in September 1990. Their reception was held on a beautiful fall afternoon in the picturesque Thelma Gaylord Forum, adjacent to the College's Bible building.

Canadian Bacon and Egg Casserole

Lynda Scott introduced Marty to this appetizing breakfast casserole. She served it for many special events in the president's home including the fall breakfasts honoring the women who worked at the University.

¾ lb. Canadian bacon, shaved
12 eggs, slightly stirred
12 oz. Swiss cheese, grated
1 C. heavy cream
½ C. parmesan cheese, grated
½ t. salt
½ t. pepper
⅓ t. paprika
¼ C. fresh parsley, finely chopped

Grease 9x13 baking dish.

Preheat oven at 425°.

Layer bacon, eggs, and Swiss cheese in greased baking dish.

Add salt and pepper to heavy cream and pour evenly across the dish.

Bake for 10 minutes at 425°.

Remove from oven and garnish with parmesan cheese, paprika, and parsley.

Return the dish to oven and cook another 10 minutes.

Remove from oven, garnish with parsley, and allow to stand for 15 minutes before serving.

Marty's Cranberry Holiday Loaf

This is one of Marty's signature recipes. She has given dozens of loaves away at Christmas and has filled many requests for the recipe. Enjoy!

2 C. whole cranberries (prefer fresh, but frozen will work)
2½ C. all-purpose flour, sifted
¼ t. salt
1 t. double-acting baking powder
1 C. sugar
2 C. pecans or walnuts, chopped
2 large eggs
1 C. buttermilk
¾ C. tasteless salad oil
Grated rind from 2 oranges (juice saved for the glaze)

Preheat oven at 350° and adjust rack to center position.

Grease 2 loaf pans (5- or 6-cup capacity) with butter; dust with unseasoned, dry breadcrumbs and tap out the excess.

Rinse and drain fresh cranberries, picking out any that are unusable. Spread on towel to dry. If using frozen cranberries, leave in the freezer until ready for use. Rinse, drain, and use frozen.

Mix all dry ingredients, including sugar, in a large bowl. Stir in cranberries, orange rind, and nuts.

Pour liquids over dry ingredients and stir to mix.

Bake approximately 1 hour, watching last 10 minutes to see that loaves brown but do not burn. Remove loaves from the pans and allow to cool for 10 minutes.

GLAZE: Combine ½ cup sugar and ½ cup orange juice and heat at moderate temperature until sugar is dissolved. Pierce top of each loaf with cake tester and use a pastry brush to spread hot glaze generously over loaves. Refrigerate before serving to set the flavors and firm the texture.

Reception Punch

Marty used a variety of recipes for punch at receptions and showers. She served it from a silver punch bowl that Carrie Lou Little Davis gave to her as a Christmas present. This punch recipe was always a favorite.

   3 C. pineapple juice, chilled
   1 qt. Sprite or 7-Up, chilled
   1 C. lime sherbet, softened
   1 C. orange/grapefruit juice, chilled

Mix all liquid ingredients in punch bowl.

Add sherbet, stirring slightly but leaving clumps of sherbet to float on top.

Add additional amounts of the same ingredients as needed, keeping proportions approximately the same.

Cream Cheese Party Mints

Anyone can buy candy mints at the store and place them on a serving dish; but here is a recipe that beats any store-bought candy and will leave a good taste in everyone's mouth.

    8 oz. cream cheese
    ¼ C. butter, softened
    2 lb. powdered sugar
    ½ t. peppermint extract
    6 drops of food coloring

Cook cream cheese and butter in saucepan over low heat, stirring constantly until smooth.

Gradually stir in powdered sugar.

Stir in extract.

Remove from heat and allow to cool.

If using more than one food coloring, separate candy dough into different pieces and add a different color to each.

Press candy dough into a rubber candy mold, using some powdered sugar to keep it from sticking to hands.

Remove candy from the mold and place on wax paper, allowing the candy to become firm.

German Chocolate Cake

After Marty's mother passed away in 1993, her father married Nancy Hufschmid. Over the years, Lloyd has come to expect Nancy's German Chocolate Cake to be served on his birthday. There is nothing better than a cold glass of milk and a piece of this yummy cake.

CAKE
1 pkg. (4 oz.) Bakers German Sweet Chocolate
½ C. water
2 C. flour
1 t. baking soda
¼ t. salt
1 C. butter, softened
2 C. sugar
4 egg yolks
2 t. vanilla
1 C. buttermilk
4 egg whites

Preheat oven at 350°.

Line bottom of three 9-inch round cake pans with wax paper.

Microwave chocolate and water in suitable bowl on high for 1½ to 2 minutes, until chocolate is completely melted (stir as needed).

Mix flour, soda, and salt. Set aside.

Beat butter and sugar in a large bowl with electric mixer on medium speed until mixture is light and fluffy.

Add egg yolks, one at a time, beating well after each addition.

Stir in chocolate mixture and add vanilla.

Add flour mixture alternately with buttermilk, beating after each addition until smooth.

Beat egg whites in large mixing bowl with electric mixer until stiff peaks form. Gently stir egg whites into batter.

Pour batter into the three pans and bake 30 minutes at 350° or until cake springs back when lightly touched in the middle.

Remove from oven and immediately run spatula between the cakes and the sides of each pan.

Allow cakes to cool 15 minutes before removing them from pans; then allow to cool on racks.

Spread coconut frosting between layers and over top of cake.

FROSTING
1 can (12 oz.) evaporated milk
1½ C. sugar
1½ sticks butter
4 egg yolks, slightly beaten
1½ t. vanilla
1 pkg. (7 oz.) Angel Flake Coconut
1½ C. pecans, chopped

Mix milk, sugar, butter, egg yolks, and vanilla in a large saucepan.

Cook and stir on medium heat approximately 12 minutes, or until thickened and golden brown.

Remove from heat and stir in coconut and pecans.

Cool to room temperature before spreading frosting onto cakes.

Executive Director

Almost eighteen years had passed since Terry succeeded James O. Baird as president of Oklahoma Christian. The College had matured during those years, having become a Christian liberal arts university. George W. Bush had spoken at the first university convocation in 1990, and two years later, his father, the sitting President George H. W. Bush, had honored the institution by addressing a thunderous crowd in the Thelma Gaylord Forum. Early negotiations were now underway to see if Oklahoma Christian would be willing to place a branch campus in Portland, Oregon. There was plenty of work on campus to keep Terry busy.

The president's house, however, was considerably quieter than it had been in many years. Jennifer and Royce had both graduated from OC and had moved to Austin, where each had begun a master's degree program at The University of Texas. Jill and Cary had just moved to Midland, where Cary began working with his father in the oil patch. Marty, in an empty nest and now cooking for two instead of four, was ripe for something new and exciting to emerge in her life.

The excitement came in the form of a brand new Mercedes sports convertible that pulled into the Johnsons' driveway on July 4, 1992. Dr. Michael Feldman, a medical doctor who had taken his undergraduate studies at Oklahoma Christian, had called Marty for an appointment. Since Dr. Feldman was a major donor to OC, Terry encouraged Marty to "see him and be nice." Accompanying Dr. Feldman was Nancy Mitchell, Marty's sister-in-law.

The meeting was brief and to the point. Dr. Feldman said that he had become an advocate for a new company, headquartered in Idaho, which sold consumable products directly to their customers. These products were healthy both for people and for the environment. He was not trying to sell any products to the Johnsons–just asking if they would consider opening an account and shopping directly with the company, Melaleuca, Inc.

With no intentions of ever telling another person about Melaleuca, the Johnsons did open their own account and began ordering from a catalog. To their surprise, both Marty and Terry found the products to be better than what they had been purchasing at the grocery stores, the discount stores, and the pharmacies. So, they continued making purchases for a few months and expressed their appreciation to Nancy and Dr. Feldman for extending them the favor.

In November, Terry and Marty hosted twenty Christian college presidents and their wives for the annual conference that rotated among the Christian colleges and universities. While Terry led the presidential sessions on campus, Marty entertained the women in her home, serving a brunch featuring her Canadian bacon and egg casserole, baked curried fruit, and banana nut bread. The conference lasted two days and concluded with a campus luncheon on Tuesday.

That evening, Terry chose to stay home and catch up on his rest, while Marty braved a cold rain to attend a meeting Dr. Feldman had arranged at Enterprise Square. The meeting featured a policeman from Florida and a dentist from Alabama. Both addressed the general topic of "why they were opening customer accounts for Melaleuca, Inc."

When Marty returned home that evening, Terry knew she was "wired." She was animated and bubbling over with enthusiasm as she related what had transpired at the meeting. This was her chance to "sing the song that was within her." Terry had had an opportunity to prove himself in his chosen profession; now Marty wanted to see what she could do on her own in the direct sales industry. "I can do this," she kept insisting.

Marty with her 1993 Mercury Grand Marquis–
the first of seven cars paid for from her
Melaleuca car-bonus checks.

After considerable discussion, Terry conceded the debate on three conditions: "No soliciting students; no soliciting faculty and staff; and no soliciting anyone inside the church building." Marty said she could work within those ground rules, and with an exception or two for very close friends, she did.

Within fifteen months of her decision to refer customers to Melaleuca, Marty had become an Executive Director with annual income that surpassed Terry's salary at the University. She still hosted university-sponsored events in her home and made the obligatory appearances on campus, but her engines were running with her new business. Nothing pleased her more than to see others who were making significant income for their own families without the risk of anyone getting hurt.

Of course, there were those who were skeptical about Marty's new business success. At best, they thought it was one of those "flash-in-the-pan" pyramid schemes. The criticisms made her work even harder. She had "the little red hen" mentality, determined to prove her detractors were mistaken about her long-term resolve.

Five years later, Marty was fifth in the nation with Melaleuca and named to the company's prestigious President's Club. Her hard work had paid off beyond her wildest dreams. Eight years after she had begun referring customers, her annual income allowed the Johnsons to begin an early retirement in the Texas Hill Country. Her Melaleuca business was an unqualified success.

In May 1995, Terry announced to the Board of Trustees that he was tendering his resignation as president but would continue to serve in the chief executive role until his replacement was named and able to take command of the University. The Board asked him to remain as chancellor following the presidential transition. He agreed and served the University another five years in that capacity.

After an extensive search, Dr. Kevin E. Jacobs was named to succeed Terry as president. Jacobs was the Executive Vice President and chief operating officer at Cascade College, the new OC branch in Portland. He agreed to begin his tenure January 1, 1996, but asked the Board's permission to live off campus in a house that he and his wife would own rather than the house owned by the University. With no one planning to use the president's house on Smiling Hill Boulevard, Terry and Marty continued to live in the home five more years while Terry served the University as its chancellor.

Melaleuca founder and chief executive officer, Frank L. VanderSloot, helps Marty and Terry burn the mortgage on their home in Horseshoe Bay

Sautéed Parmesan Tilapia

Marty's older brother, Brooks Mitchell, loves to cook freshly caught trout on the riverbanks in Colorado and Wyoming. He taught Marty this recipe on one of her summer trips to Ft. Collins, Colorado. "Bubba" would strongly recommend that you begin with the freshest white fish you can find at your local market.

> 2 lbs. fresh tilapia filets
> 1 C. Panko breadcrumbs
> 1 C. parmesan cheese, grated
> ½ C. flour
> 2 to 3 C. buttermilk
> Tony Chachere's Creole Seasoning
> Salt
> 2 T. canola oil
> 2 T. unsalted butter

Mix breadcrumbs, cheese, and flour.

Dip filets in buttermilk and coat with breadcrumb mixture.

Lightly sprinkle with Creole seasoning and salt.

Preheat large skillet to medium high; add oil and butter.

Brown each side of fish until golden brown, 3 to 4 minutes per side. Serves 4 to 6.

Italian Sausage Risotto

This recipe is the perfect complement for Sautéed Parmesan Tilapia. The balance of flavors will impress your family and your guests.

> 1 can (28 oz.) diced tomatoes, in juice
> 1 T. olive oil
> ¾ lb. sweet Italian sausage
> 1 onion, finely chopped
> Salt and pepper
> 1 C. Arborio rice
> ½ C. dry white wine
> 10 oz. flat leaf spinach, washed, stems removed, and chopped
> ½ C. parmesan cheese, grated
> 2 T. butter

Use a small saucepan to heat tomatoes with juice and 3 cups water. Bring to simmer and keep warm over low heat.

Use medium saucepan to heat oil over medium heat. Add sausage and onion, seasoning with salt and pepper. Break up sausage with a spoon and allow to brown slightly, 3 to 5 minutes.

Add rice and stir until coated and golden (approximately 5 minutes). Add wine and stir for another minute.

Add 2 cups of tomato mixture, stirring occasionally and allow to simmer over medium heat until absorbed (4 to 5 minutes). Repeat process, adding 1 cup of tomato mixture at a time, allowing it to be absorbed before adding the next. You may not wish to use all of the tomato mixture.

When the rice is tender (approximately 25 minutes), remove saucepan from heat. Stir in spinach, parmesan cheese and butter; season with salt and pepper to taste. Serve hot.

Mexican Cornbread

Here is another award-winning recipe that came from Marty's good friend Lynda Scott. It almost makes a meal in itself but is great with tortilla soup or taco salad.

3 eggs
2¼ C. milk
½ C. vegetable oil
3 C. cornbread mix (Aunt Jemima)
2 T. sugar
1 can (16 oz.) cream corn
1½ C. cheddar cheese, grated
1 large onion, chopped
2 to 3 T. jalapeno pepper slices, seeded and chopped

Grease 9x13 baking dish.

Preheat oven to 425°.

Mix all ingredients just until blended.

Bake 30–40 minutes, or until tester comes out clean and top springs back when touched.

Cut into squares and serve hot.

White Chili Chicken Soup

This is a low-fat favorite, perfect for an evening meal during the winter months.

    4 boneless, skinless chicken breast halves
    1 cup onion, chopped
    2 cans (8 oz.) white shoepeg corn, drained
    2 cans (4 oz.) chopped green chiles, undrained
    2 cans (14 oz.) Great Northern Beans, undrained
    1 t. lemon pepper
    1 t. cumin seed
    1 t. ground cumin
    1 clove garlic, finely chopped
    3 T. lime juice
    ⅔ C. Monterrey jack cheese, shredded

Add lemon pepper and cumin seed to 2½ cups water in a large saucepan and bring to a boil.

Add chicken breast halves and return to a boil; lower heat and allow to simmer for 25 minutes or until chicken is tender using a fork.

Remove chicken from pan and cut into very small pieces.

De-fat broth; return to the saucepan and add chicken pieces.

Apply vegetable oil cooking spray to a skillet; add garlic clove, cooking over low heat and stirring for no more than 1 minute. Do not burn.

Add garlic to chicken.

Sauté onions in skillet until tender.

Add cooked onions, corn, chiles, cumin, and lime juice to chicken and bring to a boil.

Add beans and allow stock to simmer until heated throughout– approximately 45 minutes.

To serve, place crushed tortilla chips and cheese in bowl and ladle hot chili over the top; serve with salsa.

Banana Nut Bread

This recipe, handed down from Mable to Marty, is a grandmother's calling card. Jennifer's boys are big fans of Mimi's Banana Nut Bread.

1 stick unsalted butter, room temperature
1 C. sugar
2 eggs
1½ C. unbleached all-purpose flour
1 t. baking soda
½ t. salt
1 C. ripe bananas, mashed
½ C. sour cream
1 t. vanilla extract
½ C. pecans or walnuts, chopped (optional)
Butter 9x5 loaf pan.

Preheat oven at 350°.

Cream butter and sugar.

Add eggs and beat well.

Sift dry ingredients and combine with butter mixture, blending evenly.

Fold in bananas, sour cream, vanilla, and nuts.

Pour mixture into buttered 9x5 loaf pan and bake for 50 miutes at 350°.

Remove to rack to cool.

Maple Family's Fudge

A wrapped box from the Maple family at Christmas time was always filled with homemade holiday candies. Marty's sister Sarah Maple and husband, Jim, passed along the Maple family's fudge recipe. If you like fudge that is smooth and creamy, you are in for a treat.

    13 oz. Hershey's Milk Chocolate Candy Bars
    2 C. real semi-sweet chocolate chips
    13 oz. marshmallow cream
    1 stick butter
    2 C. pecans, coarsely chopped
    1 t. vanilla
    4½ C. sugar
    12 oz. Pet Evaporated Milk

In a mixing bowl, break up Hershey bars, add chocolate chips and butter; set aside.

In a large stew pot, combine sugar and milk and bring to a boil, stirring constantly; allow to boil for 5 minutes.

Remove sugar mixture from heat and add chocolate and butter; stir until well blended.

Add marshmallow cream and stir until blended.

Stir in pecans and blend.

Pour into a buttered 9x13 baking dish and allow to cool.

Horseshoe Bay

J esse George was a successful businessman who had served as an executive with several oil companies during his professional career. He also served as an elder for churches in Houston and Tulsa, and was a trustee at Oklahoma Christian for ten years. Upon retiring as president of Deminix Oil, a German-owned company with its U.S. offices in Dallas, Jesse and his wife, Ann, moved to the alluring Horseshoe Bay Resort, deep within the Texas Hill Country.

One day, Terry visited Jesse and Ann to solicit their annual operating gift for the University. It was on that trip he learned that Oklahoma Publishing Company owned a three-bedroom house on the golf course next door to the Georges' charming home. Some of OPUBCO's top executives working out of Dallas used the home for entertaining their clients on golf outings. The Georges had a key to the house and looked after it during the many months when it sat vacant. They took Terry for a brief tour, and he liked what he saw.

The next time Mr. Gaylord and Terry had lunch in Oklahoma City, the subject of the house was broached. Mr. Gaylord said he remembered buying it eleven years earlier, but he had never seen the place. Six months later, the Johnsons bought the house, closing on the contract in December 1995, the same month Terry finished his twenty-one-and-a-half-year tenure as president of the University.

Marty adored her new home in the Texas Hill Country. It was slightly smaller than the residence on campus, but it was a peaceful refuge from the traffic that paraded in and out of her house on Smiling Hill Boulevard. During the five years Terry served as chancellor, Marty found herself spending more of her time in Texas. She was much closer to her daughters and to her growing brood of grandchildren, who were being delivered with some frequency in Austin and Midland. So in December 2000, after thirty-two years with Oklahoma Christian, the Johnsons took an early retirement, left dear friends and family in Oklahoma City, and made Horseshoe Bay their permanent domicile.

Among other amenities, Horseshoe Bay Resort boasts three Robert Trent Jones championship golf courses. It didn't take long for the golfing bug to bite Marty. She had always been mindful of the importance of personal physical exercise–playing tennis, swimming, snow-skiing and walking–but golf had not been on her radar screen. Now it was everywhere she looked.

At first, the game was merely a social event, when Marty and Terry could be together for four hours, sharing the moment and entertaining one another with stories about the grandchildren. Each course was a scenic delight, and the scorecard was almost irrelevant. Somewhere along the way, Marty's competitive juices kicked in, and she was no longer content playing tolerable golf.

Marty prepares to hit a fairway shot at the Fox Acres
Country Club in Red Feathers, Colorado

Marty found a golf pro that helped her improve her fundamental techniques–stance, grip, approach, swing, etc. Her swing got better, but the scores didn't go down. Then she heard of another pro that was just a little bit more knowledgeable and a better teacher than the one before. So, she tried working with him. It would take the fingers on both of her hands to count the number of golf pros that have given her lessons since she began playing the sport in earnest.

As might be expected, each golf pro suggested Marty try using a different set of clubs. She soon had a closet full of them. Her family accused her of trying to "buy" a game. Undeterred by the barbs, she made steady improvement until she finally declared herself ready to compete in the weekly Women's Day program, reserved for the Resort's best female players.

Marty's first day of competition with the ladies was almost her last. Playing a "shotgun start," she was assigned to begin her day on Slick Rock's par-five 12th hole, which is the number one handicapped hole for women. Marty, displaying a case of unsettled nerves, hit two of her fairway shots into the water and carded a 13 for her first hole of the day. It took mental toughness not to pack up her clubs and bid the ladies farewell. She stayed with the game, however, and has made a name for herself with the women of Horseshoe Bay.

Perhaps her most thrilling moment playing in the Women's Day program came on a par-three hole on the same course. Marty hit her tee shot on a precise line, 110 yards toward the pin, and watched as the ball rolled onto the green and dropped into the cup. She was ecstatic, and so were her playing partners. Unfortunately, it was not a hole-in-one. Her first tee shot had caught the lip of a creek bank and had fallen into the water. This was her second tee shot that had found the cup, and with a penalty stroke added, she carded a "hole-in-three." *Nice par.*

The biggest laugh Marty has had on the golf course was watching Terry try to retrieve one of her golf balls that had rolled into a creek that ran along the right side of the fairway. With his ball retriever in one hand and holding on with his other arm to a tree branch that extended out over the creek, Terry reached as far as he possibly could to scoop up the golf ball that was resting in the murky water. Suddenly, the tree branch broke, and Terry did a belly-flop into the creek. The rotten tree has since been cut down, but the site remains and has been dubbed the "Johnson Baptismal Gardens" in honor of Terry's unexpected immersion.

On any given day, Marty can beat Terry on the golf course. They play once or twice each week and have enjoyed playing beautiful courses all across the country. One of their favorites is Fox Acres, situated more than 8000 feet high on the eastern slope of the Rockies near Fort Collins, Colorado. The Johnsons try to play the course once each year with Marty's brother Brooks and his wife, Vickie.

In addition to the many new friends she has met on the golf course, Marty has used the game to be near to her grandchildren. Two of her grandsons are gifted with a natural swing. They always look forward to playing the game with their Mimi whenever they visit Horseshoe Bay.

Like a mother hen, Marty has the grandchildren in tow on the 14th tee box of Slick Rock at Horseshoe Bay Resort

Sunday Roast, Potatoes & Carrots

Nothing makes the house smell better on Sunday mornings than Marty's pot roast searing in a pan, ready to be placed in her Le Creuset heavy pot filled with onions, potatoes and carrots. This dish will remind you of the "good ole days."

> 3- to 4-lb. rump or shoulder roast
> 1 t. Lawry's Seasoned Salt
> Freshly ground peppercorns
> 2 T. vegetable oil
> 1 large onion, chunked
> 6 large carrots, peeled and cut into fourths
> 4 or 5 russet potatoes, peeled and quartered
> 2 T. cornstarch
> ¼ C. cold water

Preheat oven at 325°.

Wash roast and dry with paper towel.

Heat oil in large Dutch oven.

Generously salt and pepper roast.

Place fat side of roast down in hot oil and allow to sear.

Flip roast so that fat side is on top; cover and bake roast for 1½ hours

Remove roast from the oven and add vegetables; return to the oven for another 1½ hours.

Turn off oven and allow roast to sit 30 minutes in the Dutch oven before slicing and serving.

To make gravy, bring broth left in the pan to a boil; thicken broth with cornstarch mixed in with ¼ cup cold water, stirring constantly.

Aunt Lola's Rolls

Everyone enjoys homemade rolls hot out of the oven. This recipe, from Marty's dear friend Gayla Peeples, is the best of the best when it comes to quick, easy, delicious homemade rolls.

1 stick margarine, melted and allowed to cool
1½ C. lukewarm water
6 T. sugar
3 pkgs. dry yeast
2 eggs
4 C. flour
2 t. salt

Combine all ingredients; beat until thoroughly mixed.

Cover with plastic wrap and place in refrigerator overnight.

Roll out and cut for greased muffin tins.

Brush tops with melted butter.

Allow to rise for 2 hours.

Bake 12 to 15 minutes at 400°.

Summerhouse Taco Soup

The Summerhouse Restaurant in Horseshoe Bay was owned and operated by Becky Johnson. Becky's Taco Soup was the rage until the Summerhouse closed its doors. She graciously gave Marty this recipe.

> 2 lbs. ground chuck
> 1 medium onion, chopped
> 1 envelope Ranch dressing
> ¼ C. chili powder
> 4 C. water
> 1 can Ro-tel
> 1 can Trappey's Jalapinto Beans
> 1 can Trappey's Pinto Beans
> 1 can yellow hominy
> 1 large can of diced tomatoes
> ½ log of Velveeta cheese, cubed

Brown meat and onion in large saucepan or Dutch oven.

Drain or absorb with paper towels the excess liquid fat from meat mixture and stir in other ingredients. Bring to a boil.

When boiling, add Velveeta cheese.

Serve with crushed tortillas and grated cheddar cheese.

Minnesota Waldorf Salad

This salad has a refreshing taste that will complement almost any entrée. Use only Minnesota wild rice. Marty's sister-in-law, Vickie Mitchell, also adds diced grilled chicken to this recipe to make a delicious chicken salad that can be a meal of its own.

1 can (8 oz.) pineapple tidbits
2 C. Minnesota wild rice, cooked
2 Granny Smith apples, diced
2 Honey Crisp apples, diced
½ C. celery, diced
½ C. walnuts, chopped and roasted 10 to 15 minutes at 375° (do not burn)
½ C. light sour cream
½ C. Hellmann's Mayonnaise
1 T. lemon juice
¼ C. sugar

Drain pineapple, reserving 1 tablespoon of its juice.

Combine pineapple, rice, apples, celery, and walnuts.

In separate bowl, stir pineapple juice and remaining ingredients until sugar is dissolved.

Fold dressing mixture into the fruit, celery, and nuts and mix well with a spatula.

Refrigerate before serving.

Easy Bake Corn Pudding

This recipe is so easy that it almost didn't make the book. But it is so good and makes the perfect side dish for many different entrees.

> 1 can (16 oz.) whole kernel corn, drained
> 1 can (16 oz.) cream-style corn
> 2 eggs, slightly beaten
> 1 pkg. Martha White Corn Bread Mix (sweet)
> 1 C. sour cream
> 1 stick butter
> 1½ cup cheddar cheese, grated

Mix all of the ingredients except butter until blended.

Melt butter in 9x13 baking dish.

Pour corn mixture into the baking dish and sprinkle cheese over top.

Bake uncovered for 40 minutes at 350°.

If recipe is doubled, allow 1 hour to bake.

Mango and Avocado Salad

If you are looking for a salad that has great taste and stunning eye appeal, you may want to try this family favorite. It combines the best of the tropics with key ingredients normally found only in Southwest cuisine.

> 2 firm, ripe avocados, halved, peeled,
> and cut into ½" cubes
> 3 T. lime juice
> 1 firm, ripe mango, peeled and cut into ½" cubes
> Sea salt and black pepper
> 1 t. grated lime zest
> ¼ t. sugar
> 2 T. chopped cilantro
> 4 T. olive oil
> 1 can (15 oz.) black beans, drained and rinsed

Gently toss avocado with 1 tablespoon lime juice in mixing bowl.

Add mango and salt, stirring to combine.

Use a small mixing bowl to combine remaining lime juice, lime zest, sugar, and cilantro.

Whisk in oil with sugar mixture until thoroughly combined. Season to taste.

Combine black beans with dressing and stir until beans are coated.

Present salad on a small platter with beans in the center, surrounded by mango and avocado. Garnish with chopped cilantro and serve.

Baked Blueberry Oatmeal

Not only is this recipe delicious, it adds bright color and warm conversation to any breakfast or brunch. Oatmeal never tasted this good.

2 pkgs. frozen blueberries (may substitute fresh)
2 T. fresh lemon juice
18 oz. old fashioned oats
3 large eggs, beaten
⅔ C. brown sugar, firmly packed
1½ C. unsweetened applesauce
2 t. ground cinnamon
4 t. baking powder
1 t. salt
1¼ C. water
1 C. milk
¼ C. melted butter
1 C. pecan pieces, toasted

Lightly grease 9x13 baking dish.

Preheat oven at 350°.

Toss blueberries in 1 tablespoon of lemon juice and spread evenly on the bottom of greased baking dish.

Spread toasted pecans on top of blueberries.

Combine other ingredients including second tablespoon of lemon juice in a large bowl, stirring until well blended. Pour oat mixture over blueberries.

Bake, covered, at 350° for 30 minutes; uncover and bake 2o minutes more until golden brown and set.

Simply the Best Pecan Pie

Mable's pecan pie was always thought to be the world's best until Marty was introduced to this recipe from Horseshoe Bay friend Linda Offutt.

1 stick butter
½ C. light corn syrup
½ C. dark corn syrup
1 C. white sugar
3 large eggs
1 t. vanilla
Dash of salt
2 C. pecans, finely chopped
12 pecan halves
1 10" pie shell, unbaked

Heat butter in microwave or on stovetop until golden brown; do not burn. Allow to cool.

In mixing bowl, stir syrup, sugar, eggs, vanilla, salt, and chopped pecans.

Blend in browned butter.

Pour into unbaked pie shell and decorate top with pecan halves.

Bake for 10 minutes at 425°.

Lower oven temperature to 325° and bake 40 minutes longer.

World-Class Grandmother

From the moment her first grandchild was born, Marty wanted nothing more than to become a "world-class grandmother." All of her other appellations–teacher, shop owner, editor, first lady, executive director, golfer–were inconsequential when compared to being an outstanding "Mimi." No one has ever worked harder to make good on a promise to herself than Marty has in this one sphere of her life.

Two married daughters have yielded seven amazing grandchildren–five boys and two girls. Does Marty spoil them? Absolutely! She knows what they like to eat; what they like to wear; how much cash to put into their holiday greeting cards; and where to take them on special outings. They all love their Mimi.

Some people possess that gift of making each person in a group feel as if he or she is special–loved above and beyond any of the others. Marty has that gift. Each grandchild holds a special place in her heart. She was at the hospital when each was born and shared in that exciting moment when the immediate family welcomed new life into its circle. Flesh of her flesh and bone of her bone.

But the bonding she has made with her grandchildren is more about the time she has spent with each one of them during the course of their energetic young lives. She takes the two granddaughters shopping at Nordstrom's because they love the store's junior shop and the wide selection of clothing that comes in those splashy silver boxes. She takes two of the grandsons with her on the golf course–playing a few holes and then looking for lost golf balls that have been left in the rough. One of the grandsons is into guitar playing, so Mimi invites him and his friend to spend a few days each summer practicing their guitars and then putting on a concert for Mimi's friends. It's a gas!

One Christmas Terry and Marty invited the children and the seven grandchildren to be their guests on a Disney cruise to the Caribbean. The huge red, white, and black Disney's *Magic* makes one of two different circuits each week from its ocean port near Cape Kennedy, Florida, approximately one hour east of Orlando. It was the first time some of the "grands" had ever seen the ocean.

Jennifer and Royce, along with their sons, Travis, Tyler, and Tanner, left Austin a day early in order to see Cape Kennedy before departing on the cruise. Jill and Cary, with sons, Mitch and Josh, and daughters, Emily and Ashley, made their way from Midland directly to Orlando, where they were transported by bus to the ship that was waiting for them at the pier.

What is it that the poet said about "the best laid plans…"? Terry and Marty never made it to the ship before it sailed out to sea. A rainstorm in Austin caused their flight to be cancelled, and by the time they could be rerouted, it was too late to make it to the ship on time. Four grown children and seven precious grandchildren were safe and sound on Disney's *Magic*, a majestic sailing vessel, while Terry and Marty were left waving to them from the pier. Three days later, grandparents and grandchildren were reunited in Grand Cayman. She hasn't done it often in her life, but that's one time Marty "missed the boat."

The Johnson family on the Disney Cruise–January 2007
Front row: Emily and Ashley Brown
Second row: Jennifer Clark, Terry, Marty, Jill Brown
The three Mouseketeers: Tyler Clark, Josh Brown and Travis Clark
Back row: Royce Clark (holding son Tanner), Cary Brown and Mitch Brown

Marty and Terry introduce grandsons Mitch Brown and Travis Clark
to Major League Baseball in Arlington, Texas

If you asked Marty the keys to her success with her grandchildren, she would tell you that one of them is to be extra nice to their moms and dads. Her philosophy is that if you treat the daughters and the sons-in-law well, they will continue to bring the grandchildren to see their grandparents. If the kids are coming to Horseshoe Bay, Marty prepares weeks in advance, gathering the food stock she will need to deliver delicious meals, especially for the sons-in-law. They sing her praises for her work in the kitchen, anticipating each meal she prepares and the love with which it's served.

Marty has found a way to crowd a few special interests into her new life at Horseshoe Bay. When the Seton Hospital Auxiliary needed someone to serve as its president a few years ago, they tapped Marty. She drew on some of her experiences from earlier days at the College and the OCWA meetings, and the year turned out to be a great success.

When the local church in Marble Falls needed someone to teach the four-year-old Sunday-morning class, they called on Marty and her dear friend Gayla Peeples to prepare and teach the lessons. Sunday after Sunday she was down on her hands and knees, delighting the toddlers with her smile and natural gift of kindness. Her pace may have slowed slightly and her focus may have turned to other interests, but she still finds time to serve others within her local community.

Among her many personal assets, Marty's smile is the one feature that leaves an indelible impression on all who meet her. Her cheerful disposition and enthusiasm are contagious. She is a people person—a magnet for those who need a boost in life or a little encouragement to get through the day. After all, "two parts sunshine" is part of her DNA.

The last chapter of Marty's life is reserved for another time and place. She accepts each day as a gift from God and rejoices in the good that she is able to do through the strength that comes from her Lord and Savior Jesus Christ. To God be the glory.

Marty at peace in the beautiful Texas bluebonnets near Horseshoe Bay

Stewed Chicken and Gravy

This recipe is known by her grandchildren as "Mimi's all-white meal." She serves it over biscuits or mashed potatoes. Either way, it is always a hit.

> 3 to 4 lbs. bone-in split chicken breasts
> 1 T. salt
> 5 peppercorns
> 1 or 2 stalks celery with leaves
> 1 medium onion, peeled and quartered
> 1 carrot, peeled
> 1 bay leaf

Rinse chicken with cold water.

Place chicken in a heavy kettle or Dutch oven, barely covering with water.

Add other ingredients.

Bring to a boil and simmer gently for 2 to 2 ½ hours.

Remove chicken with a slotted spoon and allow to cool enough to remove all bones (watch carefully to remove even the tiny bones).

Strain the broth and save for the gravy.

GRAVY: Mix 1½ cups water with ½ cup of flour until smooth.

Bring 4 cups of saved chicken broth to a boil, adding flour mixture slowing while stirring.

Cook 2 to 3 minutes.

Reduce heat and add chicken back to the gravy.

Boboli Hamburger Pizza

This pizza is chocked full of healthy vegetables, and one piece is filling enough to make a meal. The Johnsons prefer the thin crust Boboli.

   1 large Boboli pizza crust
   1 C. of thick and chunky salsa
   1 lb. of ground round
   1 can (7 oz.) of whole green chilies
   ¼ red onion, sliced paper-thin
   1 C. five-cheese grated pizza cheese
   4 Roma tomatoes

Place pizza stone into oven and preheat at 450°.

Sauté ground round in a skillet; drain fat and blot meat with paper towels; place meat to the side on a paper plate.

Dice chilies (but not as small as pre-diced chilies in a can).

Cut onion in thin slices (almost shaved).

Slice ends off tomatoes, squeeze out seeds, then dice.

Spread enough salsa over crust to provide thin to medium coating.

Add ground round, chilies, onion, and tomatoes, spreading each layer evenly over the pizza crust.

Sprinkle cheese across the top and bake for 15 minutes. Allow a few minutes for pizza to cool before serving.

Chicken Cheese Ball

Jill's mother-in-law, Rita Brown, brought this chicken cheese ball to Horseshoe Bay for a holiday weekend. She received the recipe from her good friend Ann Adams.

    2 - 8 oz. pkgs. cream cheese
    2 - 5 oz. cans white chicken, drained
    and separated with a fork
    1 - 4 oz pkg. Ranch dressing mix
    (original buttermilk recipe)
    3 green onions, finely chopped, leav-
    ing some green for color
    ¼ C. sour cream
    1 C. pecans, chopped and toasted
       (careful not to burn)

Mix first five ingredients with electric mixer until well blended.

Roll chicken-cheese mixture in toasted pecans, using a piece of plastic wrap to shape mixture into a ball.

Wrap mixture in plastic wrap and chill until ready to serve.

Serve with your choice of crackers or rice wafers.

Dream Waffles

Marty participates in a home Bible study each week with a lovely group of women from Horseshoe Bay. Judy Standridge, a member of the class, shared this recipe with Marty, and it has been a hit with the grandchildren.

½ C. lukewarm water (105°)
1 T. sugar
2½ t. active dry yeast (one yeast packet)
2 C. whole milk, warmed to 105°
½ C. unsalted butter, melted and allowed to cool
1 t. salt
2 C. all-purpose flour
2 large eggs
2 t. vanilla
¼ t. baking soda

Eight hours before making waffles combine warm water, sugar, and yeast. Let stand for 10 minutes until foamy.

Stir in warm milk, melted butter, and salt.

Beat in flour until mixture is smooth.

Wrap bowl with plastic wrap and let stand 8 hours overnight. Do not refrigerate.

When ready to cook, add eggs (lightly beaten), vanilla, and baking soda.

Cook in waffle iron.

Aunt Vickie's Cowboy Cookies

Brooks and Vickie Mitchell, Marty's brother and sister-in-law, root for the Cowboys of Oklahoma State, the Cowboys of the University of Wyoming, and the Dallas Cowboys. Not surprising, their favorite cookies are "Cowboy Cookies."

2 sticks margarine, room temperature
1 C. sugar
1 C. brown sugar
2 eggs
1 t. vanilla
2½ C. flour (no more)
1 t. soda
1 t. salt
1½ C. semi-sweet chocolate chips
1½ C. old fashioned oats
1 cup coconut, shredded
1 cup pecans, chopped

Preheat oven at 375°.

Cream margarine and sugars together.

Add eggs and vanilla and blend.

Add flour, soda, and salt.

Stir in chocolate chips, oats, coconut, and pecans.

Shape into ping-pong-sized balls on ungreased cookie sheet, 2 to 3 inches apart.

Bake 10 minutes at 375°.

Chocolate Grahams

Okay, so this isn't exactly gourmet food, but no cookbook about Marty would be complete without her recipe for Chocolate Grahams. For years she quit making them because I couldn't keep my hands out of the cookie jar, but when the grandchildren came along, she reinstated this recipe into her repertoire. Betcha can't eat just one.

    1 stick of butter
    4 T. cocoa powder
    4 to 6 T. whole milk
    1 box of powdered sugar
    1 t. vanilla
    Graham Crackers

Melt butter with milk in a saucepan.

Stir in cocoa and bring to a boil.

Remove from heat and stir in powdered sugar to create a creamy mixture, but not loose enough to pour.

Add vanilla and continue to beat.

Spread a dollop on ½ of a Graham Cracker and cover with the other half.

Lick the bowl (my favorite part).

Recipe Index

Meats and Entrees

Beef Stroganoff	73
Boboli Hamburger Pizza	155
Broiled Beef Tenderloin	101
Canadian Bacon and Egg Casserole	116
Chicken Crepes	75
Chicken Parmesan	77
Herb-Marinated Roasted Turkey Breast	87
Italian Sausage Risotto	129
No-Peek Beef Stew	61
Pot Luck Hamburger Casserole	35
Sautéed Parmesan Tilapia	128
Sloppy Joes	50
Stewed Chicken and Gravy	154
Summerhouse Taco Soup	142
Sunday Roast, Potatoes and Carrots	140
Swedish Meatballs	49
White Chili Chicken Soup	131

Vegetables

Cornbread Dressing	89
Easy Bake Corn Pudding	144
Pinto Beans	23
Ratatouille	103
Sweet Potato Casserole	36
Twice-Baked Potatoes and Potato Casserole	62

Salads and Fruits

Baked Curried Fruit   104

Cranberry Jell-o Salad   91

Grandmother Johnson's Red Hot Apples   37

Lime Jell-o Salad   64

Mango and Avocado Salad   145

Minnesota Waldorf Salad   143

Picnic Potato Salad   51

Desserts

Apple Pie with Rum Sauce   106

Aunt Vickie's Cowboy Cookies   158

Butter Pecan Turtle Bars   79

Carrie Lou's Chocolate Pie and Meringue   108

Chocolate Brownie Nut Muffins   66

Chocolate Grahams   159

Clifford's Homemade Ice Cream   41

German Chocolate Cake   121

Gumdrop Bars   38

Jeanne's Pecan Tassies   40

Lemon Chess Pie   78

Mable's Banana Pudding   27

Manhattan Cheesecake   105

Peanut Butter Cookies   94

Simply the Best Pecan Pie   147

Strawberry Crepes   75

Texas Chocolate Sheet Cake   53

Texas Pound Cake   52

Candies

Cream Cheese Party Mints	120
Maple Family Fudge	134
Peanut Brittle	28

Breads

Angel Biscuits	24
Aunt Lola's Rolls	141
Banana Nut Bread	133
Marty's Cranberry Holiday Loaf	117
Mexican Cornbread	130
Morning Glory Muffins	92
Strawberry Bread	26

Miscellaneous

Baked Blueberry Oatmeal	146
Balsamic Vinaigrette Salad Dressing	65
Chicken Cheese Ball	156
Dream Waffles	157
Granola Supreme	93
Guacamole Dip	25
Mushroom Gravy	102
Mustard Horseradish Cream Sauce	102
Pink Salad Dressing	65
Reception Punch	119
Turkey Gravy	88